P9-ELQ-840

DISCARDED
NATHANIEL P HILL LIBRARY

Brand Bollywood

Brand Bollywood
A New Global Entertainment Order

Derek Bose

SAGE Publications
New Delhi ■ Thousand Oaks ■ London

Copyright © Derek Bose, 2006

All rights reserved. No part of this book may be reproduced or utilised in any form or by any means, electronic or mechanical, including photocopying, recording or by any information storage or retrieval system, without permission in writing from the publisher.

First published in 2006 by

Sage Publications India Pvt Ltd
B-42, Panchsheel Enclave
New Delhi 110 017
www.indiasage.com

Sage Publications Inc
2455 Teller Road
Thousand Oaks, California 91320

Sage Publications Ltd
1 Oliver's Yard, 55 City Road
London EC1Y 1SP

Published by Tejeshwar Singh for Sage Publications India Pvt Ltd, phototypeset in 11/13 Goudy OlSt BT by Star Compugraphics Private Limited, Delhi, and printed at Chaman Enterprises, New Delhi.

Library of Congress Cataloging-in-Publication Data

Bose, Derek.
  Brand bollywood: a new global entertainment order/Derek Bose
      p. cm.
   Includes bibliographical references and index.
   1. Motion pictures—India. 2. Performing arts—India. I. Title.
PN1993.5.I8B67   791.430954—dc22   2006   2006031660

ISBN: 10: 0-7619-3534-7 (PB)   10: 81-7829-692-6 (India-PB)
              13: 978-0-7619-3534-6 (PB)   13: 978-81-7829-692-0 (India-PB)

Sage Production Team: Shweta Vachani, Rajib Chatterjee and Santosh Rawat

To my wife, Bhaswati

Contents

Acknowledgements

The inspiration for this book comes from Karan Johar and Aditya Chopra. I do not know of anybody else in the Indian film industry who has so seamlessly combined the art of film-making with the business of entertainment and made a success of it. Today, if Bollywood cinema is going places and should, in the near future, emerge as a global entertainment power, the credit for providing the initial impetus would rest squarely on these two young film-making entrepreneurs.

I owe this book also to Siddhartha Dasgupta of the Federation of Indian Chambers of Commerce and Industry, Rajesh Jain of KPMG and Deepak Kapoor of Pricewaterhouse Coopers for their valuable inputs and for parting with the reports of studies on media convergence in India conducted by their respective organisations. Without their help, I could not have written this book.

Friends like Chandana Banerjee, Hemanth Vengali, Dharam Gulati, Arunoday Sharma and R. Venkatakrishnan also deserve mention for their advice and insightful comments during writing. To Raibat Basu, Vasudha Majumdar and, above all, my mother Deepika, I remain grateful for their encouragement and being beside me at all times.

I wish to thank my sister Basushree as well for uncomplainingly going through the manuscript and helping out with the research.

Introduction

I do not know who is responsible for coining the word, Bollywood. Film factotum and man about town, Amit Khanna claims to be the first to have used the expression in a news story published some time in the seventies. From whatever archival material I have been able to gather, it appears that the *Journal of the Bengal Motion Pictures Association* had coined the word, Tollywood—way back in the thirties—to describe a certain kind of 'progressive' (read 'Westernised') cinema produced by Calcutta's Tollygunge Studios. Those movies supposedly approximated the kind of productions Hollywood was then known for, only that they were not in English but in Bengali. From Tollywood came Mollywood for the films produced by the studio hub of Madras, Lollywood for the films made in Lahore, Kollywood for the films coming from Karachi, and somewhere along the way Bollywood gained currency.

The *Oxford English Dictionary* recognises Bollywood as a colloquial representation of 'India's popular film industry based in Mumbai —a blend of Bombay (Mumbai was earlier known as Bombay) and Hollywood.' As we understand, Bollywood cinema upholds a tradition of film-making replete with mindless songs and dances, star-crossed lovers, ostentatious celebrations of glamour and spectacle, lost and found brothers, convenient coincidences and happy endings. Many of us may not approve of the glycerine tears and tomato ketchup or the frenzied running around trees, the white sari drenched in artificial rain or the rising crescendo of a hundred violins. But these

are precisely the elements that have not only sustained a brand of cinema for nearly a century but have increasingly found acceptance across continents. Whether it is Aamir Khan scoring the winning run in *Lagaan* (2000) or Sanjay Leela Bhansali making a meal out of Shahrukh Khan's sorrow in *Devdas* (2002) or Karan Johar coming up with yet another three-hour candyfloss romance, audiences in London, Cape Town, Los Angeles and Shanghai are responding to them with the same emotions as those who watch these films back home in India. Indeed, Brand Bollywood going global has become a reality.

There are, of course, carping critics who debunk Bollywood as a 'wannabe Hollywood', what with a global market share of barely 2 per cent—that our ticket prices are the lowest in the world; that we are yet to produce a *Crouching Tiger Hidden Dragon* (2000); that our films are screened in rundown theatres abroad, patronised only by expatriates from the subcontinent; and that for every Hindi film released with 600-odd prints on an average, there is a *Godfather* (1972) that strikes out with 14,000 prints. In other words, Bollywood going global is just a lot of hype and hope, perhaps holding as much promise as a passable item number in a run-of-the-mill Hindi potboiler. The critics are also quick to point out that the West has never been blind to Indian cinema, whether it was Mehboob Khan's *Mother India* (1957), Raj Kapoor's *Awara* (1951), Kamaal Amrohi's *Pakeezah* (1971) or even the Mithun Chakraborty starrer, *Disco Dancer* (1982). So what's new?

The answer to this question lies in the reasons a sizzling number like 'Chumma Chumma' from *China Gate* (1998) gets transposed in a mainstream Hollywood film, *Moulin Rouge* (2001) or say, Andrew Lloyd Webber makes a song and dance out of Bollywood's extravagant cinematic traditions in *Bombay Dreams* (2002). Indians, such as Shekhar Kapur and Mira Nair are equally at home in Bollywood and Hollywood. Even otherwise, with the economy opening up in the nineties, the boundaries of Bollywood cinema are getting blurred. Unlike most other industries in India, film-making does not attract any restriction on FDI (foreign direct investment). Giant

Hollywood production houses and studios like Walt Disney, Warner Brothers, Paramount, Fox and Universal Pictures are setting up shop in Mumbai. Already, India has become an international hub for animation and special effects. Much as the Gurinder Chadha's (*Bride and Prejudice*) and the Deepa Mehta's (*Water*) make films 'with an Indian soul in a foreign body', the anxiety to reach out to a global audience at all levels cannot be overlooked. As any industry watcher will point out, never before has there been such a worldwide awakening towards Bollywood cinema and cross-fertilisation of film ideas and talent from the subcontinent. In effect, mainstream Hindi film-makers are beginning to realise that it is possible to intelligently *design* films that are viable both locally and internationally.

If we look at the bigger picture, the possibilities appear all the more exciting. Today, no producer or director, big or small, depends solely on box-office collections—both domestic and overseas—for recovering his investments. The music rights he holds can well take care of his production budget. He holds the telecast rights as well, which can again bring in substantial revenue. Then there are a host of other rights for dubbing and subtitling in languages other than Hindi, merchandising and release of promotional material, in-film advertising and co-production and distribution treaties. Taken together, the returns from all these sources can gross up to more than anything a theatre release through conventional distribution channels might possibly generate.

That is not all. Bollywood film-makers are now being presented with some never-before opportunities in keeping with global trends in the entertainment sector. Take, for instance, the mobile phone with which we are downloading movie clips, wallpapers, ring-tones and dialer tones sourced from mainstream Hindi cinema. As wireless uptake in India grows at a healthy 80 per cent annually, Bollywood has another revenue stream opening up for selling its entertainment content. Radio offers yet another lucrative option. Private FM radio broadcasters are dependent on film inputs for songs, news and current affairs as well as sponsored and commissioned programmes. Broadband Internet is another unfolding opportunity, insofar as

home entertainment is concerned. Here too, downloads of movies, songs, stills and wallpapers have become the order of the day. Internet and gaming, not to mention home video (DVDs and VCDs) as well as live entertainment have all become part of the ever-expanding spectrum of possibilities Bollywood producers are being exposed to.

All this would not have been possible, were it not for what is commonly described as the 'convergence of the media'. And driving this convergence is technology. Thus, banking on the collections of 'first day, first show' has become a practice of the past. For that matter, nobody is talking about the FSS factor these days—the planning and strategy that goes into maximising box-office receipts on the Friday, Saturday and Sunday of a film's release. Subhash Ghai may well have registered a flop with *Kisna* at the theatres in early 2005, but he has more than made up for his losses through radio and television, sale of music rights, mobile ring-tones and home video alternatives. Ditto for Ramgopal Varma's *Naach* (2004), Ashutosh Gowarikar's *Swades* (2005), Farhan Akhtar's *Lakshya* (2004), Akbar Khan's *Taj Mahal* (2006), and so on. For box-office hits like Karan Johar's *Kal Ho Na Ho* (2003), Rakesh Roshan's *Koi... Mil Gaya* (2002) and Yash Chopra's *Veer–Zaara* (2004), the returns are infinitely greater. In fact, it is very hard to lose money on films these days. If you walk down the streets of Amsterdam or are sitting in a pub at Sydney, you will hear Hindi film songs played on jukeboxes that you might not have known of till then. The films will have come and gone without your knowledge. Little wonder, many foreigners appear more knowledgeable about Bollywood cinema than most of us in India, all thanks to media convergence.

Convergence is verily a buzzword, the new *mantra* of this century. And those who have not realised this yet are bound to be left out of the biggest entertainment revolution overtaking us. With every passing day, technology is making leisure and recreational activities cheaper, more accessible, convenient and personalised. The innovations being brought about are so rapid and all-encompassing that media professionals never tire of telling us that we've 'not

seen nothing yet'. Research groups like Pricewaterhouse Coopers, Yes Bank, KPMG and Indian Marketing and Research Bureau have estimated that at its present rate of development, the entertainment industry in India would leapfrog from 4.5 billion dollars in 2005 and cross the 10 billion dollar mark by 2010. In holding a market share of 28 per cent—next only to television, which accounts for 65 per cent—Bollywood, without doubt, stands to be a major beneficiary.

Where does this leave the common man? Here, I must point out that it is economic growth, more than technology or any other factor, which becomes the prime driver for the convergence of entertainment processes. Without a qualitative improvement in standards of living, the benefits of technology will not percolate down to the masses. You may go about flashing the latest gizmo around town—even get a Shahrukh Khan to walk out live from a flickering screen (so to speak) in an auditorium—but how does it at all matter to the man on the street who is unsure of where his next meal is going to come from? Raising aspiration levels is one thing, but affordability, quite another—especially where large sections of the population are denied access to the basics of livelihood. Entertainment can thus become a cruel joke.

Fortunately, all that is changing, gradually but surely. We will again have to resort to the findings of research bodies tracking the income levels and spending habits of Indians. For instance, we have the international Goldman Sachs report of October 2003, which states that over the next 50 years, four countries—Brazil, Russia, India and China (the BRIC economies)—will become key players in the world marketplace. 'India could emerge as the world's third largest economy and of these four countries, it has the potential to show the fastest growth over the next 30 to 50 years', the report states. 'Rising incomes may also see these economies move through the sweet spot of growth for different kinds of products, as local spending patterns change.' It goes on to predict that 'the Indian entertainment industry would significantly benefit from the fast economic growth as this cyclically sensitive industry grows faster

when the economy is expanding'. As incomes rise, proportionately more resources get spent on leisure and entertainment than on basic necessities, the report adds.

There is also the Nasscom-McKinsey study of 2005 which states that leisure spending in India will be stimulated largely by the IT-enabled industry (which will generate over two million jobs) and a parallel support/services industry (creating employment for another two million people). Besides, on an average, 30 to 40 million Indians are joining the middle classes every year, triggering huge spending on mobile phones, television sets, music systems and other similar goods, following a consumption pattern typically associated with rising incomes. There are other reports as well of retail consultancies which attribute consumption spending to increasing disposable incomes on account of sustained growth in income levels and reduction in personal tax. In this, changes in rural lifestyles and their impacting the growth of the Indian entertainment sector cannot be overlooked. With its vast size of 128 million households—nearly three times that of urban India—the rural market offers yet another huge opportunity that has, so far, remained largely untapped for reasons of accessibility and affordability. Growing affluence, fuelled by good monsoons and an increase in agricultural output, have created a potential consuming class constituting 40 per cent of India's middle class and over 50 per cent of the total disposable income.

So far so good. But what these figures do not reveal (or rather disguise) are two fundamental ground realities. One, rising levels in disposable income do not necessarily lead to an increase in spending on entertainment. In fact, the contrary is true of a developing country like India. A jobless or under-employed youth is always prone to visit the cinemas, watch television, listen to music for hours and play computer games, simply because time 'hangs heavily' on him. The moment he gets busy, the finite aspect of time dawns on him. A day has 24 hours, no more. He could be earning well and improving his financial prospects, but his time-spend on entertainment gets severely curtailed. In so-called DINK (double-income

no-kids) households, where both the husband and wife are pursuing successful careers, the television set is rarely switched on. The film trade has also realised that the clientele for multiplexes (usually located in up-market residential areas) generally watch between four and seven films in a year, not because they cannot afford the inflated ticket rates, but, simply, because they do not have the time for entertainment. In contrast, traditional single screen theatres in the heart of slums and middle-class colonies are continuing to do roaring business in spite of poor projection facilities, bad seating and unhygienic conditions in washrooms. The average cine-goer at these theatres has the time to watch around 25 films in a year. How he affords it is inconsequential. The point is, all industry projections of time-spend on entertainment activities shooting up from 20 to 24 hours a week to the Western norm of 80 to 100 hours, will remain a pipe dream for the present generation of Indians.

The second dampener for any real convergence to take place is the scourge of counterfeiting. Who is not aware of the grey market for computer software flourishing right under the nose of the law? What have we done to curb audio and video piracy? How successful has Bollywood been at checking the clandestine telecasting of its films by unscrupulous cable operators? Intercepting satellite signals of Indian television channels by operators located abroad (to cater to a diaspora viewership) is the latest nuisance to torment the entertainment industry. Piracy or infringement of copyright laws is after all a borderless crime. Sadly, it is perceived as a victimless crime as well. Herein lies the crux of the problem. Unless, the industry is able to close its ranks and put in place adequate safeguards, there is no way it will be able to grow, let alone draw any advantage from the opportunities which convergence holds for the future.

On the positive side, due to the prevailing trend of moving away from analogue entertainment packages—particularly in cinema, thanks to a rise in the number of digital cinemas—much of the leakages in revenue are being plugged. For once, top Bollywood producers are venturing into individual distribution arrangements so as to claim their share which was earlier lost to piracy. The number

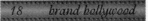

of Hindi film prints being released to overseas theatres is also rising steadily. Moreover, the emergence of professionally run international companies, who are exclusively handling Indian movies, has contributed towards an increase in the legitimate revenues of our film-makers. At present, with nearly 800 releases in a year, India holds the distinction of making more films than all the countries of Europe combined and roughly four times that of the U.S. It is thus pre-eminently positioned to call the shots in the international marketplace despite content being a perennial letdown.

This book examines these and various other related issues which affect the Indian entertainment industry on its growth path. Since cinema is a crucial constituent of this industry, my primary focus is on Bollywood—the various challenges it faces, the unfolding opportunities, new concerns, stumbling blocks, possibilities and the pitfalls it is bound to encounter while heading in the direction of media convergence. Going by past trends, the future is doubtless bright, but it is imperative to get real and not be swayed by hype in order to make the most of the new emerging global entertainment order. Another word of caution: Statistics have a way of getting dated and tend to misguide rather than inform or enlighten. So I have deliberately steered clear of fanciful figures and charts, unless absolutely necessary and verifiable. The idea is not to present a status report on Hindi cinema, but a roadmap into the fast changing entertainment landscape of India—a revolution that is bound to touch all our lives.

First Day First Show

Every time somebody talks about India being the most prolific film-making country in the world, I am reminded of the first computer game I played on my home PC years ago. It had something to do with getting a shipwrecked captain out of a dungeon in the face of mounting opposition from an array of prison guards, goblins and monsters. The captain, on his part, was equipped with several weapons, the most intriguing one being called 'fire power'. I loved it. No matter who got in his way, the captain could spray him with bullets and hop-skip his way through a maze of endless corridors with dangling ladders, free falls and booby traps. The sad part was that this fire power was limited. The trick lay in conserving the fire power and yet survive. I would invariably exhaust my fire power by indiscriminately spraying the bullets all around and my Captain Claw would die an unceremonious death!

The Indian film industry follows the same reckless logic. It streams the market with 800-odd releases every year, 90 per cent of which do not survive beyond a week at the box-office. Though nobody keeps track of the launches, on a very conservative estimate, the number is at least three times that of the number of releases. In other words, every few hours, every day, somebody, somewhere launches a feature film in this country. Before long, something goes wrong and half of them do not get completed and are aborted midway. Another 300 or so remain stillborn. In the absence of a distributor, their negatives

do not even get to leave the labs. Of the 800-odd that annually make it to the theatres, barely four or five are declared hits.

The question that begs asking is simple: Do we really need to make so many movies? Given the high mortality rate, it beats common-sense why anybody in a right frame of mind would want to invest even in a single film; considerations of social constraints and economic disparity come later. In the most affluent and industrialised countries of the West, the output is just a small fraction of ours. Yet, the market leaders are indisputably producers from Hollywood, who have been consistently coming up with around 200 titles annually for the past several decades. Bollywood also produces around 200 films annually. While Hollywood invests an estimated 3.2 billion dollars in producing these 200 films, Hindi film producers put in 3.8 billion dollars for their 200. The returns are for all to see. Not only do we have an abysmally low market share (due to the obvious language constraint), our ticket prices are not even one-tenth of what theatres in the U.S. and Europe charge. Piracy is rampant, distribution disorganised and, worse, the need gap keeps expanding at the box-office level. Perhaps, the only consolation in this in-equitable scenario is that within India, Hindi film-makers sell more tickets than their Hollywood counterparts.

In the bad old days, those who funded films were suspect. From bucket manufacturers and horse breeders to real estate developers, failed politicians and underworld dons, anybody who had money that could not be legitimately accounted for headed towards Bolly-wood. They arrived with suitcases filled with currency notes to launch a Bollywood film. It was a gamble that worked wonderfully. If the film was a hit, their status in the public eye went up to that of movie moguls. If the movie flopped, it was that much money laundered. After all, which income tax inspector was actually going to check how many cars were smashed—not to mention houses burnt and ships sunk—in the course of shooting a film? The payments made to the director, artistes and technicians, as well as for erecting sets, transport, food and lodging, were all in cash. So it was hardly

surprising that many directors who did not have a single hit to their name in their entire career, continued to make films. They were never short of work and were just burning unaccounted money.

I have known of several fly-by-night operators who call themselves producers and make periodic visits to Mumbai, but do not take the trouble of even launching a film! Bollywood has a name for these operators: proposal makers. All they do is book a hotel suite, entertain a few well-known stars with wine and women, get their signatures on a contract form (at times, for a price) and disappear the next morning. On the strength of those signatures, they are able to generate a few million from the market for films nobody would ever hear of. At the most, a launch party is held for the record and a few indoor shots canned with the stars. Then the project is abandoned for good.

Such practices still continue. But, by and large, directors and actors who matter have become wise enough not to be seen in the company of these dubious characters, at least in public. The media, too, has turned increasingly vigilant and unsparing towards the racketeers, though as late as the nineties, a star could get away with any indiscretion and never have to explain it. Directors felt all the more smug that they would never have to face the public since they operated behind the camera.

Significantly, industry output at that time had already crossed the 900-film mark and the titles registered with the Indian Motion Pictures Producers' Association (IMPPA) in Mumbai had reached an all time high of over 14,000, annually. Nobody had any clue as to who was doing what. Actors like Govinda and Anil Kapoor were doing as many as five shifts a day and Mahesh Bhatt acquired the distinction of being India's first 'director by remote control'. At any given time, he had three or four projects on the floor and he would sit at home, instructing various assistants on telephone to can his shots. Films were thus directed by proxy, in keeping with the best traditions of assembly-line production. Oddly enough, many of those films went on to become huge box-office successes.

Today, all that has changed. Govinda, Anil, Mahesh and a host of other actors and directors of the nineties have almost faded out. Bollywood too has stabilised. A certain order has been restored as stars now offer bulk dates for shoots and are increasingly restricting themselves to doing one film at a time. Instead of months and years, films are being wrapped up within weeks on start-to-finish schedules. Moreover, with the emerging of new film-making talent, the general impression gaining ground is that more than the star cast, it is the content that determines the success of films. Much as these 'new age films' are being targeted at multiplex audiences in urban centres, the very dynamics and standards of film-making in Bollywood are being re-looked.

What could have brought about this sea change? Two reasons. The first is the recognition of film-making in India as an industry. In July 2001, the government of India succumbed to the pressure of the film federation and other interested trade groups lobbying for a legal status for the industry, under the Industrial Disputes Act of 1947. Originally, the idea was to draw concessions from the government on procuring raw-stock, taxes (particularly excise and customs duty) and power consumption, as applicable to other manufacturing processes such as production of textiles, cement and steel. What came as an added bonus was the offer of some hitherto tight-fisted nationalised banks and financial institutions to fund film production. This was almost unprecedented in the annals of Hindi cinema. But there was a catch. Like any entrepreneur applying for an industrial loan, a film-maker had to go through a drill of preparing project blueprints and spread sheets, submitting audited accounts and income tax returns, obtaining insurance cover, presenting collaterals and such other documents to the bank. For those still hooked to Bollywood's anarchic ways, compliance with these procedures became difficult. So they were left out of the new dispensation. Meanwhile, angel investors and venture capitalists showed up, taking the cue from government funding agencies. Watching them, some corporate houses also jumped on to the film-making bandwagon. They all had their preconditions for releasing finance, mostly unacceptable to the old timers in film-making.

But at least, a beginning had been made at institutionalising private film financing.

The second important reason for bringing in a semblance of order in Bollywood was the advent of corporatisation. Leading production houses like Mukta Arts and Pritish Nandy Communications went public. This reduced the personal liability of the producer-promoter and, at the same time, gave him access to large sums of the share-holders' money to play with. Consequently, the stranglehold of the proverbial Shylocks, including the underworld dons, loosened. More importantly, fresh directorial talent, which earlier did not have a chance to experiment with unconventional ideas and forms, were now able to see their dreams take shape under corporate banners. Producers could afford to take risks with public money and, in turn, the directors of such *avant garde* films as *Chandni Bar* (2001), *Joggers' Park* (2003) and *Jhankar Beats* (2003) got their break. True, not all have turned out to be box-office successes, but there is no mistaking that very subtly and surely, the complexion of Hindi cinema is changing. Gone are the days when loaded moneybags, sitting sloshed in the darkness of preview theatres, could dictate terms—invariably insisting on forcing a 'wet scene' here or a rape there. The arbitrariness associated with film-making has also disappeared. Everything has become business-like. Budgets are now apportioned in advance, duties clearly defined, payments made by cheques, deadlines stipulated and everybody is accountable. Nevertheless, through all this regimentation and structuring, Bollywood film-makers have not lost their spirit of adventure. They continue to live from film to film—through the agony of failures and the ecstasy of every new success.

Perishable Commodity

While so much emphasis is placed on professional discipline and the streamlining of production processes, very little attention is paid to understanding what the audience really wants. Every

producer simply assumes that he knows what the audience expects and goes ahead to make a film. The truth, though, is that cine-goers have no expectations—other than being entertained. For that matter, they do not even wait to be entertained. It is not as though if a certain film does not get made or is delayed indefinitely, the cine-goer will feel deprived. He will choose any other film showing at any other theatre. And if he does not want to be entertained by a film in a theatre, he can watch television at home, pick up a DVD or VCD or simply scour the Internet. Today, his options in film entertainment, both legal and otherwise, are enormous, if and when he desires to be entertained.

This places the producer in a particularly piquant position. For, the moment the prints of his film leave the lab, he would be sitting on a highly perishable commodity. By then of course, he would have prepared his audience with the usual publicity blitzkrieg–trailers, posters, billboards, ads in the newspapers, radio spots, television promos and so on. As a prelude to the film release, a function for the launch of its music cassette and CD might also be held. Another common media event nowadays is getting the lead stars of the film interviewed for the press and electronic media. The more enterprising among the publicists even go around planting gossip about the cast and crew for the glossies to pick up. In addition, there would be contests, bargain offers, merchandising deals, all in order to create a buzz around the film before its release.

At times, the momentum of the campaign is sustained even after the film hits the screen, but the focus then shifts to a more substantive area of revenue collection. Here, Bollywood's famous 'territorial instinct' comes into play. Much as films are made for a pan-Indian audience, producers and distributors are known to intuitively connect a work with one or more of the six distribution territories across the country. Each of these territories is recognised by a distinct cultural identity, geographical stretch, linguistic trait, demographic character as well as the preferences and sensitivity of audiences:

1. Mumbai: This includes parts of Maharashtra, southern Gujarat and Karnataka.

2. Delhi: This covers Uttar Pradesh, Uttaranchal and the National Capital Region (NCR).

3. East Punjab: This includes the Punjab, Haryana and Jammu and Kashmir.

4. Eastern Circuit: This is made up of West Bengal, Bihar, Jharkhand, Nepal, Orissa and Assam.

5. Rajasthan: This constitutes Rajasthan, Chhattisgarh, Madhya Pradesh and northern Maharashtra.

6. South: This includes four sub-territories—Nizam, Mysore, Andhra and Tamil Nadu. Nizam is made up of parts of Andhra Pradesh and southern Maharashtra, while Mysore takes care of Bangalore and those parts of Karnataka which are not part of the Mumbai territory. Andhra makes for the remaining parts of Andhra Pradesh and Tamil Nadu comprises the entire state as well as Kerala.

Clearly, the whole of north-eastern India, including the states of Sikkim, Meghalaya, Manipur, Tripura, Arunachal Pradesh, Mizoram and Nagaland are excluded from Bollywood's scheme of things. Partly due to logistical reasons and largely due to political disturbances, Indians living in these parts do not get to see Hindi films in theatres. The farthest a film from Mumbai can reach in the north-east is the foothills of Assam—more precisely, the state capital of Guwahati.

The way these distribution territories work is quite amusing. If a film is in the nature of a crime thriller with a good deal of action, suspense and car chases, it would be targeted at audiences in the Delhi, East Punjab and Rajasthan territories. You cannot expect films like *Black* (2005) by Sanjay Leela Bhansali or *Parineeta* (2005) by Pradeep Sarkar to work in such places. If you have a musical like *Jhankar Beats* (2003) or, say, a *Page 3* (2005) with urban sensibilities,

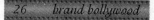
the focus would automatically shift to audiences in Mumbai and, at best, the southern parts of the country. Likewise, in case of a syrupy romance or an emotional family drama, audiences in the Rajasthan and Eastern Circuit territories become the prime targets. This explains why action films like *Soldier* (1998) and *International Khiladi* (1999) become super successes up north, but in other places, they inevitably sink without a trace. A film with youth as its central theme, such as *Dil Chahta Hai* (2001), became a resounding flop all over the country, but from the Mumbai territory alone it was more than able to make up for the losses and be declared a mega hit. Similarly, many films which run to full houses in the hinterlands falling under the Eastern Circuit are never heard of in Delhi, Mumbai, Bangalore or any of the other metros.

In the circumstances, every film-maker tries to make a mishmash of elements like action, song and dance, family intrigue, romance, comedy and suspense within a single offering—the idea is to strike as many territories as possible with one stone. Never mind if songs and dances have no place in the midst of a suspense thriller or a scene of dare-devilry interrupts a placid romantic sequence. We have seen it happen, without questioning the logic of such imperatives forced upon film-makers. Very rarely do we see these elements integrated seamlessly within a film, as in the case of a full blown romantic drama like Raj Kapoor's *Bobby* (1973) or an action thriller like Ramesh Sippy's *Sholay* (1975). These would remain landmark films in Bollywood history, not because they proved to be exceptions to the rule but for the way they could capture the imagination of an entire nation, across generations and regional divides.

Funnily, stars too have their territorial affiliations. Amitabh Bachchan and, earlier, Rajesh Khanna are among the few matinee idols who could rise above the regional level and become pan-Indian deities. Most other actors command a limited following within a localised turf. Since the mid-nineties, for instance, the Khan triumvirate—Shahrukh, Salman and Aamir—have been reasonably popular all over the country, but could scarcely make inroads into the East Punjab territory. There, the Deol triumvirate—brothers Sunny and

Bobby and papa Dharmendra—are hot. An embarrassingly inane *Kis Kiss Ki Kismat* (2004) with Mallika Sherawat cavorting with an ageing Dharmendra was a runaway success there. Similarly, in the Eastern Circuit, particularly Jharkhand and Bihar, distributors shied away from a Shahrukh Khan movie, even during his *Kal Ho Na Ho* (2003) and *Main Hoon Na* (2004) phase of 2003–2005. But pitch an old Mithun Chakraborty-starrer there and you will have ready takers any day. Then there is Anil Kapoor, who commands a sizeable following in the South and Mumbai territories, but up north, he draws a blank. Among the heroines, only Sridevi and, later, Madhuri Dixit could hold a somewhat all-India appeal—something Aishwarya Rai, Preity Zinta and Rani Mukherji have been trying to match. In any event, actresses by themselves do not make much of a difference at the box-office anywhere. This explains why Hindi films are traditionally male-centric and heroines are at best included as embellishments and, worse, play second or third fiddle to the hero.

Then there are some stars who may be very popular in India, but have no fan following abroad. Govinda, Sanjay Dutt, Akshay Kumar, Suniel Shetty, Sunny Deol and a few others fall under this category. But the three Khans are a class apart. In fact, Shahrukh's own high budget home production, *Asoka*, which bombed all over India in 2001, was rescued from being a total write-off by his overseas fan base. Ditto for *Swades* in 2005. It is this combination of domestic appeal and a growing overseas fan base that has made Shahrukh the most bankable Bollywood star of the 21st century. To an extent, Amitabh Bachchan, Madhuri Dixit and Aishwarya Rai (especially after *Devdas* [2002] and *Bride and Prejudice* [2004]) have been able to match the popularity of the three Khans in the global marketplace, but only in phases. These are important factors every producer and distributor takes into account at a time when the overseas business is expanding with every passing Friday and every new film opens simultaneously all over India and in the rest of the world.

Of late though, some inconsistencies have crept into the viewing pattern of expatriates. Their appetite for Hindi movie *masala* can

be as diverse as their palates for cuisines—ranging from the super spicy to the lightly marinated and, at times, even bland. Worse, their taste can be completely at odds with what their fellow countrymen tend to relish back home. This has been a cause for much worry among the Bollywood producers. Satish Kaushik's film on puppy love, *Mujhe Kuchh Kehna Hai* (2001), featuring a newcomer hero, Tushaar Kapoor, was a resounding success in India, but in the international circuit, it was a washout. In contrast, Suneel Darshan's family drama, *Ek Rishta–The Bond of Love* (2001), starring Amitabh Bachchan, Akshay Kumar and Karishma Kapoor, fared miserably within the country, but toted impressive collections overseas. And then, there are the success stories of *Kabhi Khushi Kabhie Gham* (2001), *Hum Tum* (2004) and *Veer-Zaara* (2004), which have been liked as much within India as by Indians settled abroad.

The clue to these inconsistencies lies in the changing tastes of the second and third generation expatriates. To their parents and grand-parents who initially set foot on foreign soil and made it their home, Hindi films were a means to connect with India. The present generation suffers from no such pangs of longing or nostalgia. For them, Bollywood is a remote concept and at the most represents a lot of *bhangra*-pop and swirling *ghagra cholis*. So any Hindi film that does not provide these basics can be very disappointing. Exceptions, of course, are *Sholay* (1975), *Pakeezah* (1971), *Satya* (1998) and *Dil Chahta Hai* (2001), which are easily understood. But give them a feudal fantasy and they would be completely at sea. Owing to this cultural disconnect, many second and third generation expatriates do not even bother to watch Indian films. (Ram Nene, a U.S.-based doctor, did not know that Madhuri Dixit was a famous Bollywood star till he married her!) The problem for our producers is that this generation of expatriates is having an increasing say in viewership choices, leading to a sudden shrinking of the traditional overseas market for Hindi cinema. This is exactly what happened to the once popular Italian cinema in the U.S. There are no takers for it today because over successive generations, Italian migrants have all become Americanised.

▓ *Delivery Platforms*

The temptation to tap the overseas market is spurred mainly by the multiplication factor of foreign exchange vis-à-vis the Indian rupee. A normal cinema ticket worth $12 in the U.S., for instance, works out to more than Rs 500, or 35 times what the producer gets on an average for screening the same film back home. Thus, producers who were till the other day sending out only three or four prints of a film abroad, have begun releasing up to 40 prints there. The general break-up is 35 per cent for the U.K. market, 35 per cent for the U.S. and the remaining 30 per cent prints for the rest of the world. But again, there are further inconsistencies. The response to a film in South Africa or Malaysia may not be the same as it is in the U.K. or the U.S. Within the U.S. itself, collections from a theatre at New York or Los Angeles can scarcely be compared to what a cinema in Boston, Dallas or Houston would generate. To imagine, therefore, that the Indian diaspora spread across the globe constitutes a homogenous, if not a captive, audience for Hindi films would be hugely misleading.

So what happens when you lose out on the exhibition front? It could be for a variety of reasons—poor judgement of the markets, wrong positioning of the film, bad timing, awful content, terrible performance of the actors, or a hostile press. Any of these factors could make or mar the run of a film at the box-office. In the past, there have been instances of producers having to sell their houses and assets to pay off debts incurred on making a film. Many shut shop and left Mumbai for good. Some are still around though, living in utter penury and complete anonymity and a few have had to switch to menial jobs. Indeed, one box-office flop was enough to spell disaster for the life and career of any producer.

This is not so any longer. Producers these days are not only smart enough to manage finances, but, like any other businessman, are also adept at spreading their losses. The most common method is

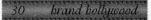

to invest in several films simultaneously in the anticipation that at least one will work and take care of the losses in the rest. It is the good old Captain Claw strategy of shooting recklessly in the dark and eventually finding a way out. From Ram Gopal Varma to Subhash Ghai to Vidhu Vinod Chopra and Yash Chopra, all the biggies in the business have adopted this tried and tested course and succeeded. The law of probability rarely lets down a film-maker who has the resources and the courage to gamble with multiple projects.

There is another way out and this applies to the small timers as well. The practice rests on the premise that when one door closes, other doors open. The box-office, both domestic and overseas, makes for the first door. The other doors, which till recently were not readily accessible, now offer a mind-boggling range of possibilities no film-maker can afford to ignore. Radio, television, mobile telephony, music cassettes, CDs, broadband Internet, home videos (VCDs and DVDs) and animation and gaming—each of these avenues represents a robust revenue stream with the potential of turning a confirmed box-office dud to an eternal money spinner. Marketing analysts describe these as delivery platforms. On another level though, each of these platforms offers the consumer an added opportunity to exercise his right to choose a medium of entertainment on his own terms. He is no longer obliged to partake in film entertainment by standing in queues and purchasing a ticket, only to be closeted in the darkness of a theatre and watch a film till its end, even as he might soon lose interest in it midway. Technology has made it possible for him to opt for film entertainment outside the cinemas. More importantly, the option grants him the luxury to switch channels, play and replay portions he likes, fast-forward what he doesn't and download what he pleases, all at his own sweet time and convenience, in the comfort of his home. For all these facilities, he is of course, supposed to pay.

Television

Arguably the biggest driver of entertainment in the future, television is currently available in Indian homes through (*i*) direct satellite, (*ii*) terrestrial channels, and (*iii*) direct to home. The monopoly of

the state-run Doordarshan (Television India) was conclusively destroyed with the advent of private channels during the eighties, most of which are now relying heavily on Bollywood cinema and film-based programmes for their entertainment and recreational content. Even channels in the niche category, such as those in the kids and news segments, are drawing upon film inputs in the form of interviews, talk shows and contests. There are also the dedicated movie channels constantly vying for telecast rights of the latest film releases, regardless of quality. As viewership ratings have proved time and again, it is not the merit of a film but its newness that determines its demand among the television channels. The next big thing waiting to happen is interactive TV. But then, in all cases, the most significant aspect about television programming in India is that growth will soon have to become subscription-driven and not dependent on advertisement revenues. This is the revenue model, which is already established in the West.

Radio

Like television, the monopoly of the government broadcaster, All India Radio, has been broken by private FM radio stations. Much as they continue to bleed owing to a debilitating license fee structure, their popularity among the youth in a very short time cannot be overlooked, largely because of their film-based programming and content. There is also the traditional AM radio, as well as the satellite and community radios (which are still at their nascent stages) for Bollywood to tap on, both as an avenue for advertising and a revenue earner. The next logical step is narrow-casting, and in time, micro-casting, which would merge with distribution channels.

Home Video

DVD and VCD systems have been around for quite some time as the most convenient alternatives to viewing the latest Bollywood releases in theatres. Little else is sold or hired out for domestic viewing. As video players will get cheaper, sleeker and better, the home theatre system will pose a serious threat to the film industry— more so, with high resolution pirated copies of DVDs and VCDs

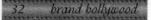

freely in circulation. In parts of the country such as the north-east, where Hindi films have very little presence, a parallel industry of counterfeit video players, cassettes and DVDs is flourishing. This contraband comes cheaper than the original and serves the important purpose of keeping everybody updated on the latest Bollywood releases. With advancements in encrypting technology and tightening of copyright laws, revenue losses from this area can be checked.

Broadband Internet

As digitisation sets into the film industry, new distribution formats on the Internet will evolve and bring about faster and cheaper modes of delivering films to consumers. Already the world-wide web has become a happy hunting ground for film buffs seeking movie memorabilia, clips, production stills, wallpapers and music. With better connectivity and rising PC penetration, this largely untapped medium will open up hitherto unimaginable revenue streams for key market players in the country. It will also define content formats and viewership patterns of consumers in the future. Online trailering is one such option. Whoever is smart enough to gauge the drift and move in first will enjoy the early bird advantage.

Animation and Gaming

This is yet another technology-driven sector where anything from movies and television programmes to mobile gaming, console gaming and Internet gaming will determine the way Indians entertain themselves. As of now, Bollywood has been able to exploit its cost advantage in the use of animation in special effects and titling of films and emerge as a major global outsourcing centre. In 2004, a brave beginning was made in the use of animation in Kunal Kohli's blockbuster, *Hum Tum*. Also, the gaming segment is making its mark internationally with the first ever investment in this industry having been made by a Chinese company in the same year. (Video gaming is big business in China, particularly in the 15–30 years age group. Since this section of consumers also accounts for the highest number of smokers, games are being devised that can

be played with one hand!) An increased number of downloads of games on mobile phones will further encourage the entry of new companies and open fresh opportunities for Bollywood film-makers. Funnily, the point at which the Indian animation and gaming industry is presently stuck is that nobody seems to know who should charge how much and from whom.

Music

Film music lends itself to a broad spectrum of activities, from cutting of albums and audio recordings for CDs, cassettes, iPods and MP3 downloads to public and private radio broadcasts, television, DVDs and VCDs, broadband Internet and mobile phone ring-tones. It can be the biggest revenue earner for any producer and, in fact, at one stage during the eighties (when there were not even half the number of options as are available at present), the sale of music rights yielded enough returns to cover the production costs of a big budget film. Today, the Indian music industry is barely able to survive, all due to widespread piracy. Despite several noteworthy measures to tackle this malady, it remains the weakest segment of the entertainment business in India. The situation is the same in other parts of the world as well. In neighbouring Pakistan, Sri Lanka and Bangladesh, piracy has almost killed the local music industry.

Mobile Phones

With an estimated growth rate of 50 million connections a year, mobile telephony is seen as the most powerful driver after television for filmed entertainment (and news) in the coming years. Till 2008 though, no major revenue inflow is expected as these are still early days for handsets. Technological innovations and advancements will raise its utility above that of merely exchanging SMS and MMS or downloading ring-tones and wall papers. Producers have already realised its potential as a non-intrusive multi-media tool, with an anytime-anywhere usage that can engage consumers in a relationship or dialogue. For instance, while promoting Veer–Zaara (2004), Yash Chopra had the automated voices of lead stars, Shahrukh Khan and Preity Zinta, answering calls made on a particular mobile

number. This resulted in an incredible 400,000 hits a day. Then, for *Swades* (2004), Ashutosh Gowarikar sent out 200,000 SMSs every day with the question, 'What would you like to do for your country?' Respondents with the best answers were rewarded with a meeting with the stars of the film over dinner. Similar interactive campaigns, polls for awards' functions and showtime contests have been yielding encouraging results. The good thing about mobile telephony is that it helps in the targeting and segmentation of audience groups (thus enabling film positioning) and, most importantly, communication is instant. The limiting factor of mobile technology is that it can work only as a pre-release build-up for a film. Nevertheless, Bollywood has already moved into mobile marketing, mobile ticketing, mobile auctions (for special shows and premieres) and issuing mobile coupons for promotions, discounts and merchandising.

▮ *Integrated Solutions*

While each of these options holds great promise, there is still a feeling of distrust, even fear, that most Bollywood producers have not been able to overcome. What happens to the good old box-office once such 'packaged entertainment' takes over? Will people stop going to theatres? The counter-argument usually tendered on this is that though people have kitchens in their homes, it hasn't stopped families from eating out. The restaurant business, in fact, is booming. So it is possible that both cinema and all related industries put together will be able to co-exist. When technology evolves, only business platforms change, but one cannot be seen as cannibalising the other. After all, no television set, DVD or VCD or mobile phone can replicate the shared experience of watching a film in a theatre on the big screen. It is, as they say, the only way to enjoy a film, just as reading a book is considered the standard for appreciating literature.

The challenge cinema faces is, therefore, not of being obliterated amidst a flurry of presumably competing activities, but of integrating

itself with these very media. Bollywood has found its strengths from this integration and is getting the audience back into the theatres. Ultimately, it is a question of capturing the mind space of the consumer, whether it is through interactive advertising, providing better viewing facilities (as in multiplexes), improving the quality of content or exploiting all available promotional tools from radio and television to mobiles, iPods, the Internet and so on. An indicator of the times to come is the way actors nowadays are effortlessly switching to producing and distributing their own films, lab owners are becoming exhibitors, and distributors are turning producers and vice versa. At all levels, film folk are closing their ranks and growing, simply by taking advantage of the emerging opportunities.

Yet another positive indicator is the revival of the studio system. Take the case of Ronnie Screwvala, one of Bollywood's modern-day visionaries, who ushered in this trend. A stage enthusiast and producer of television software, in 2004 he set up a one-stop shop to handle all aspects of film-making under one single roof—from scripting to production and direction to marketing and distribution. In less than a year, his company became so huge that it was sitting on the rights of some of the biggest titles under production—Mira Nair's *The Namesake* (2006), Vishal Bhardwaj's *Blue Umbrella* (2005) and *Omkara* (2006), Mahesh Manjrekar's *Viruddh* (2005), Rakeysh Mehra's *Rang De Basanti* (2006), Vidhu Vinod Chopra's *Parineeta* (2005), Ram Gopal Varma's *D* (2005) and Chandan Arora's *Main, Meri Patni Aur Woh* (2005). Further, he had also acquired the rights of such Hollywood productions as Robert Rodriguez's *Sin City* (2005), Louis Leterrier's *Danny, the Dog* (2005), Terry Gilliam's *The Brothers Grimm* (2005), Wes Craven's *Cursed* (2005) and Stanley Tong's *The Myth* (2006).

Screwvala's success story deserves mention, not because he was smart enough to anticipate and be the first to exploit the advantages of providing integrated solutions to the film business, but because he played a proactive role in guiding this process. For once, distributors who traditionally operated within the narrow confines of their territories saw an ever expanding market opening up. At one stroke, Ronnie was acquiring world rights of films (even before some of them were completed) and producing results. It meant taking huge risks, but with the volumes he was dealing in, Captain Claw's logic again came to his rescue whenever things went wrong. An added advantage was that he was dealing with public funds, unlike most distributors who continued to head sole proprietorships or, at best, private limited companies. Today, many market players have emerged who are following Screwvala's example and effectively re-defining the way film business is to be conducted.

What are the innovations brought about by these marketing pro-fessionals? First, the age-old practice of operating within artificially carved-out distribution territories has been discarded and has been replaced with pan-India marketing. Second, consumers are no longer regarded as individuals, but as distinct groups with common peculiarities, preferences and prejudices. The opinion of women is particularly important here, as their power in influencing negative choices is a decisive factor in group dynamics. (If a woman negates the idea of watching a particular film, the male partner usually agrees. This is not so if the situation is reversed.) Planning and strategising begins six to seven months before the release date of a film, targeted not just at Mumbai and the other metros, but covering roughly 25 cities across the country, each with a population of over one million. Passive consumers are made involved participants in these publicity campaigns and a series of promotional exercises, like concept analysis and advertising testing, is conducted, the momentum building up progressively as the release date nears. Thereafter, film content takes over and any course correction, if necessary, is carried out.

The five key points for creating such a win-win situation for the producer, distributor and exhibitor are as follows:

1. Films are not Soaps: Films are time-sensitive and have a limited shelf-life. However, this does not make them similar to other perishable FMCGs (fast moving consumer goods) in a departmental store. They need to be handled differently.

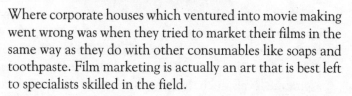

Where corporate houses which ventured into movie making went wrong was when they tried to market their films in the same way as they do with other consumables like soaps and toothpaste. Film marketing is actually an art that is best left to specialists skilled in the field.

2. Monologue to Dialogue: The secret to successful film marketing lies in taking advertising monologue to a level of customer dialogue. For it is always the buzz that a film generates that leads to word of mouth publicity. And that is what potential audiences trust, more than all the trailers, banners and television promos put together. The trick lies in scheduling a campaign in a manner that the target shifts from the unknown to identified consumers. Test screenings and consumer tracking can make this happen.

3. Competing Activities: No promotional activity can succeed in isolation and must necessarily take into account what the competitors are up to. Apart from learning from their mistakes, it also helps in developing niche strategies and, in turn, creating captive audiences. After all, no less than three Bollywood films are released every week on an average and there are some Hollywood releases also to contend with. The idea is to rise above the market clutter with the most distinctive and convincing promotional campaign.

4. Carpet Bombing: The 15–30 years age group accounts for 56 per cent of the ticket buying public. Once enthusiasm among this target group builds up, a ripple effect sets in across the board. This explains why film publicists invariably launch their campaigns with a bang in the vicinity of regular youth hangouts like college campuses, pool parlours and cafés. From there, they progressively get into bombarding the marketplace with publicity material and filling each niche as they move on.

5. Brand Building: As the life of a film extends beyond the box-office, market-savvy producers have begun talking, not of movies, but of products and brands. Brand building invariably begins with creating a 'look' for the film that audiences

can easily relate to and, in time, draw inspiration from—whether it is in the use of colours, costumes, music, lifestyle products or the language and attitude of the key characters. Publicity further reinforces these elements and raises aspiration levels, such that even if revenues are not immediate, cine-goers are at least able to differentiate the brand in the marketplace. That is more than half the battle won.

two

One Size Fits All

Which was the last jubilee hit you saw after *Sholay* in 1975? The closest comparable blockbuster that I can think of is Aditya Chopra's *Dilwale Dulhaniya Le Jayenge*, made in 1995. In the intervening years there were some mega-hits like Prakash Mehra's *Muqaddar Ka Sikandar* (1978), Raj Kapoor's *Ram Teri Ganga Maili* (1985), Sooraj Barjatya's *Maine Pyar Kiya* (1989) and *Hum Aapke Hain Kaun* (1994). Later, there were some equally huge box-office grossers like Dharmesh Darshan's *Raja Hindustani* (1996), Karan Johar's *Kuch Kuch Hota Hai* (1998) and *Kabhi Khushi Kabhie Gham* (2001), Rakesh Roshan's *Kaho Na Pyaar Hai* (2000) and *Koi... Mil Gaya* (2002), Ashutosh Gowarikar's *Lagaan* (2001) and Anil Sharma's *Gadar: Ek Prem Katha* (2001). Some might even want to include later hits like Farhan Akhtar's *Dil Chahta Hai* (2001), Sanjay Bhansali's *Devdas* (2002), Nikhil Advani's *Kal Ho Na Ho* (2003), Raju Hirani's *Munnabhai MBBS* (2003) and *Lage Raho Munnabhai* (2006), Farah Khan's *Main Hoon Na* (2004) and Madhur Bhandarkar's *Page 3* (2005). But can any of these really qualify as jubilee hits?

The fact is that Bollywood is notorious for fudging box-office figures, and in the absence of an independent audit, we can only rely on trade reports to assess the possible hits and misses. Moreover, the collection figures declared relate to a particular year and are not adjusted to inflation rates. The few millions *Sholay* grossed in 1975 would amount to several billions today. By the same token, a damp

squib in, say, 2025 would far outstrip the collections of *Dilwale Dulhaniya Le Jayenge* of 1995, but not cover its basic costs. So any attempt to draw a comparative analysis of box-office successes would be misleading. What does, however, provide a clue as to a hit or a flop is the good old standard of whether a film survives at the theatres beyond 25 weeks (silver jubilee) or 50 weeks (golden jubilee). But are we making such jubilee hits these days?

Ever since the multiplex revolution swept the country, trade analysts have come up with the expression of 'mathematical hits'. It means nothing beyond the fact that the producer has not run into losses. By their standards, if a film generates a good 'initial' by outlasting the FSS (Friday–Saturday–Sunday) criterion, it is destined to be a success. Let alone 25 weeks, one or two weeks at the theatres is good enough to recover costs in most cases. Going by the number of prints in circulation, the ticket rates and a few tax reliefs (which were not available earlier), the economics of film-making have become such that nobody waits for a 25 or 50 week run any more. Here, I am not even considering the additional revenue which tele-vision, music rights and other ancillary media exploitation bring in. The point being emphasised here is that purely on the strength of believable content it is perfectly possible to produce a good, suc-cessful movie. Should a producer take care of the following, this should not be particularly difficult:

1. Honesty: In film-making, honesty never lets anybody down. It works at two levels—honesty to the medium and honesty to the audience. The tragedy with nine out of ten film-makers in Bollywood is that they either take their audiences for granted or resort to gimmickry in order to cover up their inadequacies. The film medium allows them this license. Respect towards audience intelligence automatically elimin-ates a great deal of narrative flaws, unwanted frills, technical flourishes, attention-grabbers and superfluities that eventu-ally work against a film. This explains why most modern films that are high on style but low in content never work at the box-office. The cine-goer, however motivated, is no fool and

can see through the intent of a film-maker within the first 15 minutes of a screening. Give him a routine love story, even in black and white, and with plenty of rough edges, if narrated with sincerity, he will accept it. A film with several high jinks, sound and fury but ultimately signifying nothing will promptly be rejected. Honesty infuses a film with raw energy that crackles through every frame.

2. Narrative Style: It is a fallacy that the audience always expects something different or original from every film. If there is novelty in the content, it is most welcome. If not, nobody ever holds it against the film-maker. Sarat Chandra Chatterji's novel, *Devdas*, was made into a film almost a dozen times, but when Sanjay Leela Bhansali tried doing it once again in 2002, it was widely accepted. Why and how it happened lies in the narrative style of the film-maker. Mehboob Khan made *Mother India* in 1957, which was actually a remake of his earlier film, *Aurat* (1940), and it proved to be more popular than the original. Thereafter, the same theme has been regurgitated countless number of times with different focal points and protagonists, which has led to the creation of classics like *Ganga Jamuna* (1961) and *Deewar* (1975). Audiences did not tire of the later versions just because they had seen the original. In 2001, as many as five films were made, almost simultaneously, on the freedom fighter, Bhagat Singh. But the one featuring Ajay Devgan in the title role ran to full houses purely on the strength of its treatment—the narrative style. Likewise, in 2004, two films based on the same Hollywood source, *Unfaithful* (2002), were released in the same week. While *Murder* succeeded, *Hawas* did not, again for the same reason—narrative style.

3. Star Line-up: Film-making is about teamwork. Along with high profile actors in the cast, the crew and the rest of the artistes and technicians in a production unit contribute their skills and reputation to create a brand value for the film. Till the fifties, these people used to be employees of production houses drawing fixed salaries by the month. With the

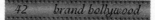

demolition of the studio system, freelancing became the norm and stars began to call the shots. Even then, association with a banner or production team determined their mass appeal and even success. The RK banner boasted of writers like K.A. Abbas and Jainendra Jain, poets Shailendra and Hasrat Jaipuri, the music composer duo Shankar–Jaikishan, cameraman Radhu Karmakar and sound recordist Alauddin. Dev Anand's banner, Navketan, had its own set of loyalists, like cameramen Fali and Jal Mistry, lyricist Sahir Ludhianvi, music composer Sachin Dev Burman (and later his son, Rahul Dev Burman) and so on. Today, with the focus shifting to stars, 'camps' have come up. Shahrukh Khan belongs to the Karan Johar camp (or vice versa), just as Urmila Matondkar and, later, Antara Mali became part of the Ram Gopal Varma camp, while Sanjay Dutt finds himself in the Sanjay Gupta camp. Call them loyalists or lucky mascots, together they constitute a winning team that every distributor would like to back.

4. The Element of Sex: Nothing sells like sex in cinema. It is the oldest trick in the film-maker's book to lure audiences to the theatres. But there are censorship laws that make it so much of a forbidden fruit. Whether it is Mandakini's famous bathing scene in *Ram Teri Ganga Maili* (1985) or Mallika Sherawat's much-hyped 17 kisses in *Khwaish* (2003), a soft-porn actress performing a rape scene or bare-bodied men outdoing women in a skin flick, there can be no end to the flights of fancy a film-maker embarks on in total defiance of the censors' strictures. It is a cat and mouse game the film industry and the government have become accustomed to playing for over a century. The good part is that Bollywood has progressed well beyond the stage when physical intimacy had to be depicted by two goldfish in a bowl or parakeets pecking furiously at one another, interrupted suddenly by the outburst of a fountain!

5. Bending the Rules: Nothing is sacrosanct in film-making. If songs and dances were a must at one time, today they are not. Likewise, the customary cabaret, bedroom scene, lost-and-

found brothers and a host of tired cinematic clichés are being questioned by a generation of young film-makers and audiences alike. Today, it is a brave new world out there where predictability and monotony are being spurned. Whoever treads the tried and tested path reaches nowhere. But then, the indications were there all along, whether it was Prakash Mehra foisting a hero who never smiled or ran after girls in *Zanjeer* (1973) or Sooraj Barjatya making a home video of an Indian wedding in *Hum Aapke Hain Kaun* (1994) or Ashutosh Gowarikar breaking the jinx of sports films with the highly entertaining *Lagaan* (2001). These were all super-hits. Modern pressures of cost-cutting, speedy single-location shoots and professional accountability have also contributed to the trend of film-makers checking for options off the beaten track.

6. Financial Prudence: Common-sense dictates that for any enterprise to survive, costs must not exceed returns. In the earlier days, producers gambled with their savings and invested in films without knowing whether their work would find any takers and, if so, for how much. Today, only fools operate in such conditions of uncertainty. In the first place, nobody invests his personal savings in such a high-risk, big-budget business without the basics being covered. More often than not, the film is pre-sold to distributors at the budgeting stage and the smarter producers even make 'table profits'. In this manner, the risk is spread out and in the eventuality of a flop, no single producer, distributor or exhibitor has to bear the entire burden of loss. There are many other ways they get to hedge their bets. It is all a matter of how cleverly you juggle your finances and are able to maximise profits without having to stick your neck out.

7. Publicity Build-up: For everybody in the film industry, publicity is oxygen. Good or bad, it keeps you in the limelight and ensures the longevity of your career. Whether it is an unfounded rumour, speculation of being romantically linked with a star, a court case, gossip about a domestic crisis, censorship controversies or hard news about production schedules, the

public always has an appetite for such sensational *filmi* stories. Add to this a gullible press that allows itself to be manipulated. Even a planted story is promptly lapped up. On a serious note though, it always makes sense for a film-maker to keep the pot on boil and feed the media with information on the launch of the film, progress of shoots, music releases, corporate tie-ups, promotional contests, clarifications on controversies and celebration parties. At times, an award can revive the prospects of a film, as it happened with Bimal Roy's *Bandini* in 1966. The film had run its course and was about to be pulled out of the theatres when, out of the blue, came the announcement of *Bandini* bagging the President's Silver Medal and six Filmfare awards. Miraculously, it gave a fresh lease of life to the film.

8. Creative Accountability: A quick glance at Bollywood's history will reveal that in nine out of ten successful films, producers have doubled as directors. Whether it was Raj Kapoor or Dev Anand, Guru Dutt or Bimal Roy, Manmohan Desai or Prakash Mehra, Yash Chopra or Karan Johar, the hand that held the megaphone also controlled the purse strings. Even in the case of Ram Gopal Varma, every time he made a film, the possibility of curning out a flop was much lower than when he allowed another director to step in or when he himself directed for another producer. The reason for this is that whenever Varma wore the dual cap of producer and director, he was emotionally accountable only to himself and no-one else for all the money and creative inputs that went into a film. His anxiety always was to maximise his ROI (returns on investment). Since an outside director holds no direct stakes, he could well be getting on with a 'job to be done' and not bothering to look back thereafter. It helps a great deal if the director is made a stakeholder in a production so that he not only puts in his creative best, but he also becomes financially accountable for all lapses. Such active involvement is necessary because it is neither possible nor desirable for the producer to direct his own film every time or be present on the sets throughout the duration of a shoot.

▦ Vanishing Formulas

One may also count inspired story-telling, an objective approach and even blind luck as factors which could contribute to the success of a film in some measure. But these are not as important as the eight points mentioned earlier. What we have identified are the key elements that make for a fixed matrix, which influences a favourable response from the audience towards a film. Honesty, financial intelligence, creative accountability and publicity support are, of course, the basic criteria that are common to all kinds of films made. But if you have a film that is as run-of-the-mill and predictable as *Veer–Zaara* (2004), you will need to compensate for the weak storyline with a strong star line-up. In a film which is high on sex, like *Jism* (2005) or *Murder* (2004), you can do without stars and still pull off a hit. Likewise, you might have a film with a team of freshers but which scores high on the story content and publicity support. Again you have a hit. Ultimately, things have to even out one way or the other within the matrix, if a film has to run. And should all the eight elements be taken care of, there is just no way that a film should turn into a flop.

It is not as though producers and directors are unaware of these elements of a successful film. The trouble is that most of them usually get so carried away with the excitement of launching a project that their priorities get mixed up, or they tend to be so lazy (or unduly optimistic) as to remain blind to obvious lapses. They do not see the eight components of the matrix to be closely interrelated and would rather deal with any one or two of them in isolation. In effect, what usually emerges is a film that may be star-studded but lacking in substance, or a film that is strong in story and scripting, but with little else for support. Rarely do we find a film that competently orchestrates all the elements and thereby leaves a lasting impression in the minds of the audiences. Some such noteworthy exceptions are Raj Kapoor's *Awaara* (1951), Mehboob Khan's *Mother India* (1957), K. Asif's *Mughal-e-Azam* (1960), Abrar Alvi's *Sahib Bibi Aur Ghulam* (1962) and Ramesh Sippy's *Sholay* (1975).

These films were made under trying conditions, with not even a fraction of the facilities present-day film-makers enjoy. Film-making technology (as we know it today) was then at its primitive stage. Besides, there was no support from television and there were no DVDs, VCDs, music cassettes, Internet or mobile phones. With all the odds stacked against them, these stalwarts still managed to produce perennial hits.

What prevents us from producing such classics now? A simple, most obvious and convenient explanation would be that the level of commitment and, by extension, working standards in the industry have fallen. Also, it may be argued that audience expectations have gone up. On further examination it might be argued that the dynamics of the film industry have changed so dramatically that those earlier projects can no longer be viable if they were to be remade today. The truth is that the quality of film-making, both conceptually and technically, has only improved over the years, not deteriorated. Also, if there is still an audience for a coloured version of *Mughal-e-Azam* (1960), and *Sahib Biwi Aur Ghulam* (1962) can be made again (not to mention *Parineeta* and *Devdas*), obviously there are takers for these classics. And third, the scale of film-making has expanded so much and opportunities for distribution have multiplied to such an extent that, on purely budgetary terms, handling those early films would actually be child's play. Bollywood has matured to a point where it holds the capacity to handle any kind of film, of whatever magnitude and budget to match the very best in the world. The point is what stops it from going all out? Why should it continue to operate below its potential?

The answer lies in the death of the formula. Films can no longer be made with a one-size-fits-all approach because audiences are sharply divided. Growing film literacy and exposure to overseas cinematic trends through the electronic media have created this strange scenario. On the one hand is that section of the public that still abides by the principle of 'willful suspension of disbelief' while watching films, and on the other is the section that is not only discerning and demanding but has built an intellectual firewall around itself. In the past, an intelligent film-maker could successfully

penetrate that firewall (whenever and wherever it existed) with a formula that appealed to the collective consciousness of the masses. So there were the *Hunterwali* (1935) type of 'Fearless Nadia' films, the Rajendra Kumar kind of weepies, Manoj Kumar's patriotic sagas, Manmohan Desai and Prakash Mehra entertainers, and even the David Dhawan sort of coarse comedies. These were all formulaic stuff that worked well as they had a homogenising emotional appeal on audiences. In Mehboob Khan and K. Asif's time, the formula worked even better because film literacy had hardly set in and audiences were all the more receptive.

The advent of film-makers like Karan Johar, Ram Gopal Varma and Madhur Bhandarkar segmented the market into the mainstream and the niche. Today, any film-maker who is unsure of himself targets the niche market and somehow manages to square his accounts. The ambitious and confident, like Yash Chopra and Karan Johar, have been going mass and are pulling off bigger hits. Subhash Ghai, for all his seniority and stature, felt left out at one stage and targeted the mainstream market with *Yaadein* (2000) and *Kisna* (2005), misfiring on both occasions. The risk element in the mainstream is comparatively higher because budgets are huge and the focus is diffused. Niche, in contrast, allows the film-maker to play it safe, with ideas and feelings and not be compelled to make either spectacular or feel good films. Small wonder then that Sanjay Leela Bhansali went all out to splurge on *Devdas* (2002) but with his next film, *Black* (2005), he became severely restrained, because it was a niche audience he was consciously catering to. On both occasions he scored. Likewise, when Ghai acquired the rights of a small film, *Iqbal* (2005), he launched a new company to handle its distribution, and his marketing strategy also changed. Sure enough, he scored a hit this time. Such understanding of the market and, in effect, deciding on the positioning of a film can make the difference between success and failure. Very rarely does a film like *Lagaan* (2000) or *Dil Chahta Hai* (2001) rise above the level of niche and become a mainstream hit.

Of late, two ultra-niches have emerged. One is the Mahesh Bhatt variety of skin flicks carrying a quality tag (as distinct from the

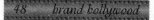

undisguised sleaze of C-grade porn movies). The other is the low-budget but high-on-concept films targeted at the multiplex audiences in urban centres. With as many successes as failures in both cases, the relevance of the formula is being brought to question again. For every *Khwaish* (2003), *Jism* (2003) or *Murder* (2004), there has been an equally disastrous *Sheesha* (2005), *Rog* (2005) or *Chaahat Ek Nasha* (2005). For every multiplex hit like *Jogger's Park* (2003) or *No Entry* (2005), there is a *White Noise* (2004) or *My Brother Nikhil* (2005) biting the dust. Farah Khan may have set an example with *Main Hoon Na* (2004), but another feel good romance like *Socha Na Tha* (2005) bombed. Likewise, a *Munnabhai MBBS* (2003) has the nation cracking up in laughter, but another comedy like *Padmashree Laloo Prasad Yadav* (2005) became a damp squib. Even tried and tested action thrillers, revenge dramas, war films, period epics and ghost stories are no longer safe propositions.

The problem, as any trade analyst would explain, is that Bollywood is yet to outgrow its herd mentality which leads to a situation where formulas are repeated to the point of overkill. Another explanation is that all formulas are based on the conventional theory of dramatic conflict—a clash of opposites—inevitably good vs evil. Scriptwriters can scarcely see beyond this point. They have always been trying to foist a convincing evil figure for the hero to take on, be it a terrorist, landlord, smuggler, politician or a dacoit. Little do they realise that such stock villains have become passé. The audience would much rather see characters with shades of grey than have to make value judgements of good and evil. It is for this reason that films with no identifiable villains, such as Karan Johar's *Kuch Kuch Hota Hai* (1998) and *Kabhi Khushi Kabhie Gham* (2001), turned out to be runaway hits.

▨ Market Research

But then, as they say, trends in Bollywood move in cycles. An idea may be irrelevant today, but tomorrow the timing might just be

right. The reverse is also true. The idea by itself never dies; only that it must await its time. Had *Page 3* (2005) or *Black* (2005) been made in the seventies or eighties, in all likelihood they would not have even found distributors. *Jai Santoshi Maa* (1975) made box-office history in the seventies, but today it cannot be expected to survive beyond a week. Similarly, several flops like *Line of Control* (2003), *Tango Charlie* (2005), *Elaan* (2005), *Main Prem Ki Diwani Hoon* (2003), *Chingari* (2006) and *Fight Club* (2006) could well become huge hits in the future if re-released at an opportune time, and *Black* (2005) could be a dead disaster. Sadly, in a hurry to produce clones of the last big hit, most film-makers lose sight of this fundamental fact—timing of the release. The intention of every producer always is to play safe, recover costs and move on. But the impression everybody else gets is that our film-makers have run out of ideas.

Part of this problem could be resolved if there are independent market research bodies advising producers on their projects since the very inception. In the West, there are specialised consultancies run by marketing professionals who advise the studios at every stage on the dos and don'ts of making and distributing films. They assess the suitability of a project, its strengths and weaknesses, the kind of competition it is likely to encounter, the opportunities that the market offers and how best to exploit them. Accordingly a comprehensive distribution plan is drawn up with details of the pre-release publicity schedules, co-ordination between the media, release of prints, international premieres, branding exercises and so on. Even minor details like supplying movie stills to the press and arranging interviews with the cast and crew are taken care of by the marketing agency as part of a promotional build-up. Nothing is left to chance.

In India, we are still stuck at a stage when the film-maker invites the families of his cook and chauffeur to a trial show before calling in the distributors. The reaction of cooks and chauffeurs is supposed to be a more accurate barometer of public response than the polite murmurs of friends and colleagues. This drill worked in Raj Kapoor's and Bimal Roy's time. The closest we have now got to market research

is inviting sample groups to preview screenings and eliciting their 'approval' on a scale of one to ten. How accurate the exercise can be is evident from Vinod Khanna's experience with *Himalayputra* (1997), the film he funded to launch his son, Akshaye Khanna. It was awarded a rating of eight out of ten, whereas at the box-office it turned out to be a Himalayan disaster. Another film which was released around the same time, *Dilwale Dulhaniya Le Jayenge* (1995) (which marked Aditya Chopra's directorial debut), was given a rating of 2.5, but it went on to create an all-time record of a 500-week run in a single Mumbai theatre, Maratha Mandir. Even otherwise it is ranked as one of the biggest hits in Bollywood history.

These instances have only lent substance to the film industry's standard argument that market research is a total waste of time and, worse, nullifies creativity. What these cynics do not understand is that there are far more intelligent ways to gauge the pulse of the people accurately than rely on the opinions of friends or families of chauffeurs and cooks or, for that matter, sample groups. Market research becomes all the more important in India considering the diverse and fragmented nature of audiences, the multiple options of entertainment opening up, the influence of lifestyle products, religion, fashion, rising affluence, shifting demographic patterns and, most importantly, the need to derive the first mover advantage. A good researcher is able to easily pick up early murmurs in the market, feed information about audience preferences into the creative process, maintain camera diaries, conduct workshops and discussions and recommend strategies for promotion and publicity. Effectively, he produces a 'predictability barometer' so that the film-maker knows the returns on his investment in advance. The element of risk-taking becomes so much more reduced.

After all, every viewer who walks into a theatre carries with him a baggage of expectations based on what he knows and feels about the film he is about to see. The inputs he gathers from friends and other sources as well as what he remembers from watching earlier films on the same subject also contribute to what might be described as his benchmark for evaluating the film in question. Any film-maker privy to this crucial piece of information at a macro level has a

winner in his hands. All he has to do is amplify the theme of his film in relation to the collective benchmark—perhaps flesh in some fresh ideas or tinker with the storyline—and move the audience from a state of expectancy to the level of a pleasant surprise, shock or intrigue.

The role of market research is to influence the creation of a benchmark among the audience through a variety of means—publicity material, launch announcements, official news releases and even feeding the gossip mills. Perception formation about the film is thus tracked, challenged (if necessary) and shaped simultaneously so that everybody is cued to the intended image of the film. In the West, trained moles are let loose in public places like college campuses, shopping plazas, parties and railway stations to manipulate public perceptions. At times, street interviews can provide vital clues on how the film is shaping in the minds of potential viewers. Some of the key questions raised at this stage are: Are the promos engaging enough and easy to remember? Is the focus of interest on the star cast or on the message? Does the communication hold recall value? How persuasive or impacting is the campaign? Depending on the responses, periodic brainstorming sessions are held with the director and his unit, with the intention of doctoring or editing the film according to need. Only after making the final cut are representative audience groups called in for a trial show.

Here again, during the trial show, the methodology followed is far more foolproof than anything Bollywood has known. In the preview theatre, each viewer is given a rotary dial marked from −100 to +100, with zero at the 12 o'clock position. All dials are hooked to a central computer which records the responses of the sample group. To register a negative response to a shot or scene the pointer is turned left in the −100 direction and for a positive reaction, it is turned in the +100 direction. Being neutral or indifferent is indicated by the pointer in the zero position. Some market research groups are known to install close-circuit cameras around the auditorium, whereby scene-by-scene reactions of the sample audience are captured and superimposed on the screen while the film is rerun at the evaluation stage for the production unit. When correlated with the responses registered by the rotary dials, the findings would track the 'peak' and 'ebb' in interest levels during the course of a screening. To many this may appear a tedious exercise, but its utility as a means for identifying the strengths and weaknesses of a film is obvious. Cues to initiating corrective measures, both within the narrative as well as in the promotional campaigns, would also emerge from this very basic exercise.

Missing Links

Bollywood's reluctance to invest in research stems from its deep-rooted suspicion of any homogenisation of information. The one-size-fits-all analogy again comes into play here. For one, India is such a vast nation with so many layers of social, cultural and economic issues that any attempt to present a cohesive picture of audience likes and dislikes could be misleading. For another, the complexion of the entertainment industry is changing so rapidly that at no point in time are film-makers able to keep pace with the implications of the developments. The options that are available today to consumers of entertainment will inevitably be overtaken by something new tomorrow. In fact, most film-makers have just given up, not even bothering to take stock of the existing facilities which could possibly impact their own business. They would rather play the proverbial ostrich with its head firmly stuck in the sand than be concerned with anything beyond the creation of film content and form.

Here is a quick low-down of the missing links in Bollywood's understanding of emerging opportunities in the film business:

Digital Cinemas

The future of cinema lies in the development of digital technology. With heightened picture resolution and quality, minimal distribution costs and quicker delivery time for prints, it promises to raise box-office collections exponentially. However, at present, the initial

investment on digital projectors and making theatres adaptable to the new technology is a forbidding factor. Even so, thanks to initiatives taken by entrepreneurs like Manmohan Shetty, Jawahar Goel and Bharat Shah, India could boast of over 100 digital cinemas in 2005. Of these, 65 are already operational and another 65 are due to come up within a year in the southern parts of the country. This is just indicative of how fast conventional celluloid is being replaced by digital prints and changing the way Indians take to cinema. Opinion is, however, divided on whether this would check piracy. Only time will tell.

Digital Film-making

Closely related to digital cinemas is digital film-making. Although the Super 35 technology does not afford a major cost advantage at present, improved print quality and the prevailing trend towards digitisation is prompting some film-makers to opt for it. Ketan Mehta claims credit for making India's first complete digital film, *Mangal Pandey: The Rising*, which was released in 2005. The alternative to this is that the film is shot normally in 35mm and then, at the post-completion stage, it is converted to a digital format and released along with the special effects. Some of Mumbai's premier labs are digitising at least one film a week. Some films to have been distributed digitally include Nikhil Advani's *Kal Ho Na Ho* (2003), Kunal Kohli's *Hum Tum* (2004) and Farhan Akhtar's *Lakshya* (2004).

EDGE Technology

This is a facility to stream movies on the mobile phone, provided, of course, that the handset has the necessary features and is so enabled. All that a subscriber needs to do is visit the cellular operators' website through the handset and click on the link for the movie of his choice. Management guru-turned-film-maker, Arindam Chaudhury claims to be the first in the world to have made use of this technology in 2004 for his film, *Rok Sako To Rok Lo*. Those who wanted to see it on their handsets had to go through the pre-specified drill, thanks to a tie-up Chaudhury (as producer-director of the film) had with a mobile company. As an additional

inducement, he offered the service before the film was released in the theatres. Even then there were hardly any takers, simply because not everybody possessed the particular handset model the film-maker had in mind. This must, however, be seen as a teething problem. Very soon, mobile handsets will be standardised and enabled for streaming movies at no additional cost.

Animation

Using animated (or cartoon) characters in live action films is nothing new. However, Bollywood film-makers, for some inexplicable reason, have not explored this possibility to the fullest extent. (In television commercials though, ad film-makers have regularly been using them.) In 2004, Kunal Kohli laid the ground for animation in Hindi cinema with *Hum Tum*, wherein the characters, 'Girl' and 'Boy' became as much of an integral part of the film as its lead actors Saif Ali Khan (playing a cartoonist) and Rani Mukherji. The animated characters instantly caught the imagination of the public, prompting the producers to try out several innovative marketing formats, such as, running comic strips in leading newspapers and introducing them in some popular television serials like *Jassi Jaisi Koi Nahin* (2003). Animation received a further boost when Shahrukh Khan broke convention and lent his voice for the dubbing of the Hollywood blockbuster, *The Incredibles* (2004), in Hindi.

IMAX

Although a slow starter, the IMAX format is steadily gaining ground in India. When the first IMAX dome came up in Mumbai, it held more curiosity value than an experience people would like to savour time and again. Moreover, the movies screened (*Alaska: The Spirit of the Wild* [1997], *Apollo 13, 2001: A Space Odyssey* [1995] and *Everest* [1998]) were in the nature of educational films, prompting critics to comment that their appeal would not extend beyond school children. Indeed, in the initial stages, busloads of school kids patronised the shows on block bookings. Over time, Hollywood blockbusters in the IMAX format, like *Spiderman 2* (2004), *The Polar*

Express (2004) and *Robots* (2005), were released, thereby changing the audience profile. IMAX theatres have since come up in Hyderabad, Ahmedabad, Delhi, Kolkata and Jaipur. Very soon, Bollywood film-makers will be making their own IMAX movies, rather than let Hollywood imports draw full advantage from its rising popularity in India. Bharat Bala's Aishwarya Rai-starrer on the legendary romance between Emperor Shah Jahan and Mumtaz Mahal offers a case in point. Many others are to follow.

Home Video

The home video market is turning out to be the next big source of revenue for Bollywood films. With an unprecedented boom in satellite television and the overseas market, home video rights have shot through the roof, from an estimated Rs 0.5 million per movie to well beyond Rs 10 million. This approximates the price a producer normally gets from one distribution territory for a moderately budgeted film. What is more, old classics are finding a new lease of life in the DVD/VCD format. For instance, in 2004, the VCD version of *Sholay* (1975) was one of the biggest legitimate hits in the home video circuit with over 200,000 copies sold within the year. Yash Raj Films also got into the domestic video market following the international success of its productions, *Hum Tum* (2004) and *Veer–Zaara* (2004). Ravi Chopra's *Baghban* (2003) was another major money spinner, which turned the fortunes of a small video library (that acquired its rights) into a multi-million rupee company. India, however, is yet to catch up with the international norm of the home video market generating two to three times the revenue of box-office sales.

NRI Funding

Non-Resident Indians patronising Indian films abroad is old hat. What's new is the huge resource pool they have come to represent, following U.S.-based IT baron, Kanwal Rekhi's investing in Bollywood. Today, financing Hindi movies in Mumbai is a rage among Silicon Valley professionals and their families and friends. Vivek Wadhwa, who co-founded two IT companies, produced

My Bollywood Bride (2006). Krishna Pillai, a software executive, and his wife, Renuka, chipped in U.S.$ 1 million to produce Mahesh Manjrekar's *Padma Shree Laloo Prasad Yadav* (2005). Likewise, U.S.-based techies, Raj Nidimoru and Krishna D.K., invested in two Indo-American projects, *Shaadi.com* (2001) and *Flavors* (2003). Much as these films have not set the box-office on fire, the recognition of Bollywood's potential as an attractive investment destination is indicative of better times to come for our film-makers. Once these overseas investors come to grips with the way film-making works in India, the floodgates of finance will open up for just about everybody.

The Multiplex Revolution

The growth of multiplexes might have been negated (in numerical terms) by the closure of single screen theatres, but as a cinematic experience its appeal to the young urban Indian is very encouraging. It has opened the market for small budget movies catering to niche tastes and has ensured healthy returns for film-makers. Moreover, with their ability to drive footfalls consistently into large format malls, multiplexes have fuelled an unprecedented retail boom all over India. But the biggest blessing they hold (largely unexplored though) for exhibitors is the new window of opportunity for non-film entertainment—sporting events, awards functions, music concerts and beauty pageants. It is only a matter of time before producers and distributors are able to devise ways to leverage this opportunity to promote their films.

Crossover Cinema

In spite of being a much-maligned and much-misused expression, it has been the dream of every Bollywood film-maker to produce that one international hit on which he could blow his trumpet for the rest of his life. The first to get anywhere close to achieving this was Shekhar Kapur with *Bandit Queen* (1994) in the mid-nineties. But that was for a British producer. Mira Nair's *Monsoon Wedding* (2001) was in the same league. Meanwhile, there have been some creditable attempts to invade the West by regular Bollywood dream merchants like Aditya Chopra (*Dilwale Dulhaniya Le Jayenge*), Karan Johar

(*Kabhi Khushi Kabhie Gham*), Ashutosh Gowarikar (*Lagaan*), Nikhil Advani (*Kal Ho Na Ho*) and Yash Chopra (*Veer–Zaara*). The others continue to grapple with a mishmash of Hindi and English in the mistaken notion that the hybrid language would help connect better with overseas audiences. Some are now making two versions— Hindi and English—simultaneously, as Subhash Ghai and Ketan Mehta did with *Kisna* (2005) and *Mangal Pandey: The Rising* (2005), respectively. The idea is clearly to reach out to an audience well beyond the Indian diaspora. Bollywood may still be waiting for a *Crouching Tiger Hidden Dragon* (2000) or *Life is Beautiful* (1997) to emerge from within, but the real crossover will take place the day Shahrukh Khan shares the lead with a Brad Pitt or Nicole Kidman, or Aishwarya Rai (or any other mainline actress) becomes, say, Tom Cruise's heroine. That day is not far.

Foreign Players

Just as Indian film companies are diversifying and turning public, there are also the foreign distributors (who already had a presence in India) who are getting into the integrated mode by combining distribution with production and exhibition activities. As the economy opens up and with no caps on foreign direct investments (FDIs) in films, things can only get better. Many are already holding dual portfolios of Hollywood and Hindi films and, to an extent, ploughing back their profits into financing Bollywood productions. For instance, Sony Pictures of India (formerly Columbia TriStar) could notch an estimated Rs 1 billion in 2004 simply on the strength of its huge portfolio and aggressive marketing of its films across all markets. While others may wait and watch or still be testing the waters, the writing on the wall is very clear: Collaborate, consolidate and co-exist. The days of cut-throat competition are over.

three

Distribution Is God

If content is king, distribution is god. So it must be said of the movie business. No matter what a film is about or how it might eventually look on screen, if it has not been marketed well, all is wasted and you will inevitably be left with a turkey in your hands. And no matter what anybody might have to say about the quality of Bollywood cinema, the fact remains that we sell more tickets than any other country in the world. This just goes to prove that there still exists a burgeoning market for the song and dance routine of mainstream Hindi cinema. Despite this, if Hollywood studio owners are world leaders at the box-office today, it is not because they produce uniformly superior films. Much of what they churn out is of bad quality, but they manage to get away with it because of better language reach and, more importantly, a supremely aggressive marketing machinery. This hasn't been easy for them anyway. For one, it costs much more to produce a film in Hollywood than in India. For another, ticket rates are at least 10 times higher in the English-speaking world than they are in India. So what they are doing actually is selling a far more expensive product for a higher price than we do. In effect, even as we continue to outperform the U.S. by over 50 per cent in terms of the number of admissions, we are unable to take advantage of low production costs and ticket rates. The average rate of admission across India (not just the metros) is a miserable Rs 15 per ticket—lower than even Africa, Latin America, the Middle East, Singapore and the rest of the Asia-Pacific region.

There is surely a lesson somewhere to be learnt in all this. With an annual turnover of less than a billion U.S. dollars on an average, we may never be able to match Hollywood's record of grossing close to 10 billion dollars a year. But should we be able to reach at least the half-way mark, it would greatly transform the perception the world has of Bollywood cinema. The obvious way to go about this is by identifying our strengths and weaknesses as a global player. But before getting into that, it would help to take a leaf out of Hollywood's recent experiences and perhaps figure out how different we are in our approach to the business of film-making:

Sequels

Hindi film-makers are scared stiff of producing sequels and would rather turn out remakes and copies of proven hits from the past. In the U.S., it is the other way round. From the *The Lord of the Rings* series (2001, 2002, 2003) to *The Matrix Reloaded* (2003) to *X-2: X-Men United* (2003), *Shrek* (2001) and *Spiderman* (2002), every major hit has had a sequel snapping at its heels. It is as though every time a film-maker runs out of ideas, he leans back on a recent success and produces a sequel. The strange part is that these extended versions turn out to be just as successful as (if not more than) the originals. This completely negates the notion that Bollywood film-makers have nurtured about sequels leading to comparisons with the original and eventually falling short of audience expectations. It is the reason why Ramesh Sippy, despite pressure from all quarters, never tried to make a *Sholay 2*. Other film-makers who do occasionally venture into making sequels of earlier hits choose to camouflage the effort with new titles and, possibly, a different cast and crew.

Day-'n'-Date Release

In the U.S., the trend now is to ensure that a film releases internationally on the same day as its domestic opening. This not only provides a huge boost to box-office revenues but also serves as a catalyst for the growth of the home video market. On the flip side though, even the most successful films have shorter overall runs as

they typically exhaust their audience faster. It is a chance worth taking considering the numbers that are generated on a large opening weekend. Somehow, Bollywood film-makers have been reluctant to take these chances, at times choosing to premiere their films abroad months before the date of domestic release. At other times, the films are subjected to a staggered release across the globe, again for no plausible reason. The best thing about international day-'n'-date releases is that it limits the chances of piracy cannibalising box-office collections.

Holiday Weekends

Every producer or director knows that the best time to release a film is on the weekend when it does not clash with another big-budget feature. And if it is an extended weekend preceded and/or succeeded by holidays, competition can get very intense. In the U.S., such holiday weekends are regarded as 'prime property' and studios actually go around bidding for the best theatres in advance to get their films released during the period. Such practices happen here in India too, but what we haven't yet become wise to is the possibility of releasing films on a Thursday or Wednesday if it is a holiday and, particularly, when two or more big films are scheduled for release simultaneously. (Of late though, some multiplexes in Mumbai are pulling out flops a day or two in advance and substituting them with a new film on select screens.) In the West, this is being increasingly tried out and the results are hugely encouraging. A five-day opening with a Wednesday release not only generates a terrific buzz, but it also minimises the chances of a bloodbath at the box-office. Dussehra and Diwali holidays are ideal occasions to try out this possibility.

Freebies

The simplest and surest way of luring audiences to a film is by offering freebies—a cap, T-shirt, popcorn coupons, dolls, toys, etc. —and billing them to the publicity budget. Hollywood studios are even offering free DVDs of movies to sell theatre tickets of their sequels, as in the case of *Spiderman 2* (2004). Those not making sequels are distributing CDs of television promos and excerpts of forthcoming films produced under the same banner. Such freebies cost only a fraction of what is usually spent on mainstream advertising (television, billboards, etc.) and go a long way in the brand building of a film. In India, we still tend to be miserly about investing in these token giveaways, despite the prices of cassettes and CDs crashing in recent years. The best we have done so far on this count is gifted popcorn and *samosa* coupons and held lotteries of cinema tickets (which nobody trusts). And then, it is not the producers but exhibitors and owners of multiplexes who announce such schemes to fill up the seats.

Interactive Gaming

In 2004, Warner Bros became the first Hollywood studio to establish an in-house video game division and publish its own game. *Matrix Online*, a massive multiplayer online game (MMOG) was developed. Much as Bollywood production houses will regard these activities as diversions from their mainline business, the essential benefits emanating from them cannot be ignored. This is just one way to illustrate how film brands can, after all, generate parallel revenues from other activities. It is only a matter of making the most out of every available opportunity.

Home Video

DVDs have revitalised the home video market in the U.S. and, in turn, added to Hollywood's overall revenue pie. Producers are able to garner larger shares from the sale of video rights, particularly when release windows (the time gap between the release of a film and its video) are getting shorter. In India, the same conditions prevail, only that our attitude is different. We still believe that home video, if encouraged, could grow into a monster and eat into the box-office market. We do not realise that the two mediums actually complement one another and, together, can constitute the best weapon to beat piracy. From time to time, the Film Federation of India, at the instance of distributors and exhibitors, has been placing meaningless embargos on the release of video and satellite rights

for specific periods. So long as it suits the producer, he will abide by the embargo; otherwise, in all likelihood, he will just not bother and nobody can do anything about it. In the bargain, the sell-through market for DVDs has not been able to develop, while the rental business, despite the poor picture and sound quality on offer, is thriving. With declining hardware prices, the situation is likely to be reversed and, like the West, DVD penetration should improve.

Online Rentals/Downloads

Much of Hollywood's movie business is conducted on the Net, particularly through online rental schemes. For a nominal monthly subscription, film fans are entitled to receive unlimited copies of DVDs on rent and, in some cases, simultaneous rentals as well. DVDs are delivered to subscribers at their doorstep along with pre-paid return envelopes. Some companies have also started offering movie down-loads on the Internet. The only problem Indians face in both cases is their inherent suspicion about cyber security. Rather than disclose their credit card details on the Net, they prefer to deal with someone across the counter and pay in cash or cheque. Besides, downloading movies from the Internet is time consuming, even with broadband.

Much of the movie-making world has begun following Hollywood's examples as 'best practices' in the trade, if only to promote domestic cinemas. India is an obvious exception. Thus, while the box-office collections of the EMEA (Europe, the Middle East and Africa) countries combined are fast catching up with Hollywood's turnover, India seems caught in a cesspool of its own making. The third important region, the Asia-Pacific (excluding India), is also going great guns, having already crossed the half-way mark, thanks mainly to the protectionist policies of Japan, China, South Korea, Singapore and Taiwan. For instance, China does not allow imports beyond 20 films per distributor per year, but has an ongoing arrangement with Warner Bros for the production and distribution of U.S. films, besides setting up new theatres, digital cinemas and IMAX theatres. Australia, however, is different. It is served with more screens than required and is now engaged in converting existing facilities to digital theatres for cinema advertising prior to the screenings of the main

feature. Apart from price increase, there is little scope for box-office growth in these parts.

Growth Drivers

Like most of its neighbours, India too had a protectionist policy till the mid-nineties when a series of measures directed at liberalising the economy was set into motion and changed everything in film business and trade. Restrictions on the Motion Pictures Exporters Association of America (MPEAA) were lifted; the wings of the state-owned National Film Development Corporation (NFDC) were clipped and its role as India's sole canalising agency for films ceased; and free trade in films was encouraged. Consequently, any-body can import any film into India and, subject to censorship laws, screen it whenever and wherever he pleases in the country. Similarly, there are no special approvals required any longer for exporting films. What is more, the government has entered into treaties for preferential treatment with countries like Italy and Canada. Many more are to follow. This progressive breaking down of trade barriers between India and the rest of the world has contributed to the growth of Indian cinema in no small measure. At the international marketplace, India would thus appear to be living up to its age old credo, *Vasudhaiva Kutumbakam*—The World is One Family.

Other obvious growth drivers for our cinema are as follows:

Regional Cinema

Films made in Tamil, Bengali, Marathi, Malayalam and other regional languages of India are no longer marginalised or in any manner regarded as lesser than mainstream Hindi or Bollywood cinema. (Uttar Pradesh also makes Hindi films.) Mainstream Hindi cinema may be topping the production charts with an output of 200-plus films annually, but Telugu cinema is fast catching up and Tamil, Kannada and Malayalam are not far behind. In fact, Bollywood

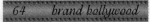

film-makers are hugely inspired by films in these languages, both stylistically and for story ideas. The influence of Bengali and Marathi has been no less. And for the record, the state of Maharashtra (in which Bollywood is located) stands at a modest fifth position in the list of density of cinema halls, while Andhra Pradesh and Tamil Nadu are the toppers. It is just that by virtue of Hindi being the 'link language' of the country, Bollywood manages to garner 40 per cent of the market share in terms of box-office revenue every year.

Very soon, this too will change. Film-makers in regional languages have turned increasingly market savvy and are outgrowing the narrow confines of their traditional viewership base. What started with a few actresses, like Padmini and Vyjayanthimala moving over to Mumbai and Bollywood starlets Khushboo and Naghma setting up base on the other side of the Vindhyas, has now become a full-blown exercise in cross-fertilisation of talent. Preity Zinta and Rani Mukherji are as much at home in Chennai as Priyadarshan and Mani Ratnam are in making movies in Mumbai or Kolkata. Aishwarya Rai and Abhishek Bachchan are acting in Bengali movies, just as Kolkata-based Rituparno Ghosh is drawing actors and funds from Mumbai. A Hindi hit like *Munnabhai MBBS* (2003) gets made into Tamil as *Vasool Raja MBBS* (2004) and Kamal Haasan tries to make each of his films in as many languages as he can. In fact, bilinguals and multilinguals have become big business, for better or for worse. What is noteworthy here is not the desire to reach out to a nation-wide audience, but the necessity to connect with a growing viewership of Indians settled abroad. For the regional producer, this results in increased scalability in terms of content and access to newer geographies. For the investors, it means de-risking their investment by widening their audience portfolio.

Dubbing

Just as regional films are dubbed in Hindi and vice versa, dubbing of international hits into Indian languages has become fairly routine, if a somewhat questionable practice. Many are critical of the practice of dubbing on the grounds that it, more often than not, kills

the spirit of the film. Yet, since the late nineties, every major Hollywood fantasy has found a Hindi expression, whether it is *Jurassic Park* (1993), *Anaconda* (1993), *Titanic* (1997) or *Spiderman* (2002). In 2004, *Spiderman 2* was dubbed in three local languages, and with 305 prints in circulation, it went on to break all box-office records of dubbed Hollywood films released in India. On several other occasions—particularly in respect of action films—dubbed prints have fared better at the box-office than their English originals. The reverse is also true. But the prevailing attitude in the market is to have more dubbed prints in circulation and limit the exhibition of originals to mainly metropolitan centres.

The reasons are obvious. The business generated by dubbed films is growing by the day, whereas response to English versions has reached a plateau. Nobody in a small town or village could be really concerned if the audio goes out of sync and the expressions of the spoken words do not match the visuals. This is a peculiar problem with translating into Indian languages, as the verb usually appears at the end of a sentence, while in English it occurs much earlier. A better option would therefore be to run subtitles, but, for obvious reasons, they would never work in India. In the circumstances, we are making the best of a bad situation and viewers are not complaining. The fact is Arnold Schwarzenegger has become as much a house-hold name in India as Rajnikant is in Japan, thanks to the reach of dubbed prints.

In-film Advertising

Today, nobody is surprised if an actor on screen orders a soft drink by name, or a motorbike of a particular make is shown repeatedly, or a scene is set in the showroom of a reputed home appliance company. In this age of sponsorships, everybody knows and understands. No matter how disturbing the effect might be, we realise the compulsions of a film-maker to blatantly plant or play upon brands, rather than blur or camouflage them as was done in the past. After all, in-film advertising is now considered a substantial revenue source for film-makers strapped for cash. For advertisers, movies

guarantee a captive audience, unlike television, which has the capacity to show more commercials but does not guarantee viewership. For audiences, association of a brand (mainly lifestyle products) with a superstar raises their aspiration levels and could even prompt purchases. It therefore becomes a win-win situation for all. Of late though, advertisers are turning pretty demanding and choosing only those films that conform to the sensibilities of their target customers. Desperate film-makers will go to the extent of not just tweaking their scripts, but changing the entire storyline if that ensures an advertisement bonanza. The day is not far when some movies would turn out to be full-length commercials, featuring mainline stars and made entirely on the advertiser's money.

Merchandising

Indians are slowly waking up to the promise that promotional items hold in transforming the fortunes of films. From *Superman* (1988) and *Batman* (1989) to the latest fantasy thriller, Hollywood's marketing whiz kids have not spared a single opportunity at peddling life-sized dolls, masks, costumes of characters, junk jewellery, belt buckles and other assorted movie memorabilia in the market. Apart from providing publicity, they also bring in the big bucks. The earliest and most visible example of a Bollywood film exploiting this opportunity was *Koi...Mil Gaya* (2002), when tiny replicas of the extraterrestrial character, *Jadoo*, appeared in toy shops around mid-2004. By then the film had already run its course and no real advantage could be derived from the sale of these items. For a Hollywood film, merchandising usually gathers momentum two months prior to the release date, beginning with people dressed as characters of the movie moving around in shopping malls and parking lots. The farthest we have got to in promoting a Bollywood film is by hawking T-shirts and caps bearing its title and, perhaps, the star cast. Things don't work this way in modern India.

Multiplexes

The growth of multiplexes has ensured a platform for movies that appeal to niche audiences who can afford to pay the inflated admission

rates for better exhibition facilities and ambience. After all, exhibition is said to be the last mile in the film value chain when the patron interacts with a film. Deplorable conditions in conventional single screen theatres had turned away a large section of cine-lovers, including family audiences, from the cinemas. Now they are all going to multiplexes, not just for the superior viewing experience, but also for the benefits of shared facilities within a complex, like food courts, book stores, gaming parlours and so on. Many multiplexes actually rely on food and beverage sales as revenue generating avenues and have gone beyond the conventional coke and cold *samosas* to offering sugarcane juice, tender coconut, doughnuts and pastas. Other than that, revenues are generated through concession stands, ad sales (launch of new brands) and commercial tie-ups between, say, a hi-fashion boutique and a jewellery designer in promoting a film. But the biggest blessing of a multiplex is optimal capacity utilisation for screenings. For one, the multiplex operator has the flexibility to decide upon a screening schedule, depending on the duration of each film, so as to maximise the number of shows in a day. For another, he is able to maximise the revenue potential of every film by juggling around with prints for different screens, depending on the seating capacity of each hall. Typically, after the first or second week of its run, a film is moved into smaller halls, making way for a newer release in the larger halls. It ultimately works out to more shows, better occupancy, clever cost management and, naturally, higher profits.

Distributors' Dilemma

From the many opportunities opening up, it would appear that distribution is the safest and most lucrative enterprise in the film business. But is it really so? Does not the producer enjoy the privilege of skimming off the best part of revenues before anybody else? Having a unique vision and playing by the cuff is one thing; surviving in the marketplace and sustaining profits on a regular basis is quite another. How do you ensure that your film stands out in a clutter of releases during the week? What is that 'extra something' you are carrying into your film that makes it special? Where do you find your core audience and how assured are you of its loyalty? Consumer patterns are forever changing. A number of other variables also come into play which are beyond your control. Things just do not happen the way they should. You could be expecting the delivery of your prints on a certain date, but they don't arrive. The censors could be sitting on them. The lab technicians could be on strike. The financier could have run out of money and an actor who hasn't been paid could have brought a court injunction on the film's release. In Bollywood just about anything can happen any time. And yet we are producing workable films. This is because everybody is fired by high optimism—hoping for the best and preparing for the worst.

The roadblocks an Indian distributor faces in his line of business are far too many to recount, but some problems are common. The most fundamental is that the distributor does not know who he is catering to. He is perpetually on a blind date. His target audience could be so fragmented as to belong to one or more of the six layers of the economic classification—from the super rich to the ultra poor—and he has to apply the same marketing tools regardless of how the producer would like to position the film. As we shift from the analogue to the digital mode of distribution, things get even more complicated. Under the analogue system, the production and packaging is undertaken at one end, while distribution is done by a third party. But in the digital system, a framework of interoperability automatically falls into place whereby business systems get linked to content generation. Effectively, distribution becomes integrated into the media value chain with no third party intervention or added costs.

But the distributor has a choice here. He can either upgrade his operations from being a mere dispenser of prints to becoming part of the value chain—appropriately a producer. That way he gets to create, manage, distribute and deliver the film to the consumer.

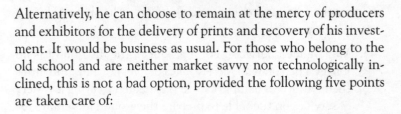

Alternatively, he can choose to remain at the mercy of producers and exhibitors for the delivery of prints and recovery of his investment. It would be business as usual. For those who belong to the old school and are neither market savvy nor technologically inclined, this is not a bad option, provided the following five points are taken care of:

1. Adversarial Role: Gone are the days when producers and distributors shared an adversarial relationship with one constantly suspecting the other's intentions. It used to be a silly 'snake and mongoose fight' with neither emerging the winner. Today, both have to be extremely trusting and accommodating towards one another and, as equal partners in the business, need to be totally transparent, especially in their financial dealings.

2. Poor Quality: Lack of knowledge about the technicalities of film-making is no excuse for compromising on quality. For that matter, producers aren't expected to be competent directors, cameramen or computer geeks. Basic awareness about prevailing film-making standards is good enough for raising the bar so that unit members, both artistes and technicians, know exactly what is expected of them.

3. Limited Finance: An extended value chain adds to costs. Typically, at any stage, the distributor spreads his finance across three or four films, the returns on which could be staggered over time. If this 'rolling of money' gets inordinately delayed or the film turns out to be a non-starter, he could be out of business. In the absence of safety nets in the industry, he must have deep pockets in order to survive.

4. Market Intelligence: A distributor is in a more privileged position than the producer (or director) at gauging the market's pulse. By virtue of his place down the value chain, he is the first to spot an opportunity and can guide a production team into tailoring the product accordingly. That way everybody gets the early bird advantage. Such possibilities depend entirely on the alertness of the distributor, how he

catches the market buzz and the rapport he shares with his producer.

5. Value-added Services: For a producer, the distributor is no longer a person who merely takes delivery of cans and farms them out to his exhibitors. He is expected to bring a variety of services on the table to prepare the ground for a film's release so that the market looks forward to it with a heightened degree of anticipation. Essentially, he has to not just spot but create opportunities for a film's successful run in the box-office.

The question that arises now is obvious: What prevents a distributor, who is both knowledgeable and capable of doing so much, to directly get into production? Why does he need a producer in the first place? Similarly, it can be argued that in this time and age, why does a producer need a distributor? There are also contentious issues of delayed schedules, breach of trust and equitable revenue sharing to be dealt with at every stage. Clearly, beyond adding to costs, intermediaries down the delivery chain have virtually no role to play. With digital technology coming in, they have become all the more redundant. Significantly, the Barjatyas had shown the way long ago. So today, when distributor-exhibitors like Manmohan Shetty or Shrawan Shroff take to producing movies, and traditional producers like Yash Chopra and Ronnie Screwvala turn to distribution, the reasons are understandable. In a competitive environment, there is just no room for cost-enhancing practices and conventions that have exhausted their utility. In a nutshell, the advantages of combining production with distribution are as follows:

Complete Control

From conception to final delivery, the producer assumes complete control over the life of a film. He has absolute authority in deciding its fate—how it is to shape up, the content and quality, pace of production, release date, marketing and promotions. He is answerable to himself and no-one else, for all these decisions. Most importantly, he is not at the mercy of intermediaries, who could only be raising his costs and causing delays.

Manoeuvrability

A producer-distributor is uniquely placed when it comes to navigating through roadblocks, even when it means revising his own decisions and not having to consult anybody. Cutting corners, trouble shooting, crisis management, risk taking and coarse corrections become easier when the buck stops at his table. The biggest advantage, though, is that he can plan his publicity well before the launch of a film because he alone knows what exactly to expect of it.

Financials

Traditionally, production used to claim an estimated 88 per cent of a film's budget (on an average) whereas marketing and distribution had to make do with the remaining 12 per cent. Today, a ratio of 72:28 appears to be the norm. When the producer distributes his own film, the tendency always is to be more liberal with allotting funds for promotion and publicity. He knows that apart from his own profits, he stands to earn what he would have otherwise had to part with as the distributor's share.

Piracy

The more number of hands a film passes through, the higher the chances of piracy are. Monitoring the movement of prints becomes virtually impossible whenever multiple distributors and their agents come into play. Even today, film prints are transported, unguarded, in railway compartments and public vehicles. With digitisation and built in safety measures like encryption and security locks, the producer is in a better position to take charge of any exigency and check counterfeiting.

Credibility

As the creator of a film, the producer carries far more credibility in the eyes of the public than a distributor. No matter what the latter says in favour of a film, he is always regarded as a salesman anxious to peddle someone else's product. Even television channels do not give him any importance. He cannot have the same passion or

conviction in his exhortation that a producer has. Cine-goers find it easier to identify with and listen to a producer than a distributor.

The biggest challenge in the distribution business today is that of raising ARPU (average realisation per unit) levels. While the market has already enforced a streamlined value chain, it is yet to provide digitised addressable networks at prices affordable to all. Technology could well come up with viable solutions for the future. Till that happens, film-makers will have to grapple with complexities of extending the shelf-life of their films, be it through television, Internet, mobile phones or any other media. Each of these holds huge promises and poses as many problems in the distribution business. How Bollywood can possibly exploit them to its advantage is dealt with, at length, in the next few pages.

◼ Video Boom

Let us start with the boom in video, cinema's closest cousin. Indians have outgrown the stage when they had to put up with pirated copies of films in scratchy video cassettes rented out by the day. Today, new Bollywood releases can be watched in the comfort of the drawing room on sleek VCD or DVD players, with CDs which are cheap, easy to store and produce better picture and sound quality. Barring the usual distractions and disturbances in a home, it is the nearest a family can get to the cinematic experience of a big screen. In parts of India like the north-east, it is the only cinematic experience the present generation has known ever since insurgents shut down theatres screening Hindi films. Even otherwise, in many middle-class households in metropolitan centres, watching films at home is a regular practice because it costs less to rent a DVD/VCD than visit a theatre with the family. In exceptional cases, should a film be particularly appealing or popular, the family sets out to the theatre. To that extent, the video serves the purpose of a film trailer.

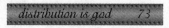

Another reason for the popularity of home videos is an unusual crash in the prices of VCD/DVD players. Till the late nineties, only the very affluent could afford them as the prices were more than Rs 20,000 per unit. Owning a home video system was considered a status symbol in those days. Then, in 2002, China-manufactured VCD players entered the market at a price of about Rs 1,800 a piece. That was when large scale video penetration into small towns across India took off. Promptly, major electronics giants operating in the countryside slashed their prices by almost three-fourths. What is more, these companies started bundling the players with television sets, washing machines and other consumer durables to make them an attractive buy for the rural consumer. Today, in the grey market, a non-branded VCD player can be obtained for as little as Rs 1,000— almost what an average middle-class family would otherwise budget for towards an evening out at a multiplex in the city.

There are two ways for Bollywood to look at this phenomenon. One is to acknowledge the fact that there can be no stopping the market from joining forces with technological advancements. The other is to resist change on the ground that video is eroding the vitals of the film trade. Distributors and exhibitors have always accused producers of being excessively greedy, arguing that by selling their video rights within days of a theatrical release, they are putting the former out of business. Producers argue that an extended release window will only amount to sending out an open invitation to pirates to invade the market. This is too high a risk for the film industry to take, more so with potential revenue streams from a proliferation of satellite and cable channels. In the circumstances, it is better to make peace with the video industry and develop a relationship of interdependence rather than an adversarial stance. The main issues at stake here are as follows:

Growth Potential

Notwithstanding its perceived popularity, home video hasn't captured even half the market it should have by now, going by its potential. In 2004, an estimated 5 per cent of Indian homes owned VCD/DVD players. This worked out to barely 10 million units.

According to market researchers, the figure should have well crossed the 25 million mark, given the growing affluence of Indians, rising aspiration levels among the youth and the popularity of related lifestyle products. Moreover, the easy availability of large-screen television and LCD has brought the film-viewing experience closer to that of movie theatres. Screenings at classroom theatres, movie clubs, corporate seminars and workshops are all making use of the large screen facility. In time, information on the cost-benefits and other merits of these gadgets should percolate down and render market penetration more effective.

Acquisition Costs

Several home video distribution companies are now supplying content to cable operators and television channels. Significantly, nothing sells as well as film-based entertainment—not sports, education, travel or tourism. Even hard-core news channels are now purchasing footage on star interviews, music videos, song contests, awards' functions and film parties from video distribution companies. The highest demand is, of course, for full-length feature films—the newer the better. While many may regard the overdose of Bollywood on the small screen as a dilution of serious programming, the fact remains that it is film content alone which generates the highest viewer ratings and ad revenues for the channels. So nobody minds paying more to video companies for acquiring telecast rights of these programmes. Also, producers are in a better position to demand their price from video companies, and for all concerned, everybody makes a good pile at the end of the day. Above all, it amounts to so much more revenue generated for the film industry.

Music Companies

The collapse of the music industry (in the face of piracy) during the late nineties has prompted several key players to now diversify into selling home videos of films. Essentially, these companies are buying the music of films together with its video rights and using their distribution and marketing networks to retail them. As is well known, Indian music companies enjoy the strongest and most extensive

marketing network in the entertainment business. So, it suits the producer perfectly when he enters into such package deals. For the music companies, the video not only provides an additional source of income, but also helps to couple their marketing and acquisition costs. Combined promos, merchandising and conducting contests for both movies and music have helped these companies bring down costs even further.

Goonda Act

In 2004, the state government of Tamil Nadu took the unprecedented step of imposing the Goonda Act on video pirates. Almost miraculously, video piracy in the state was eliminated, and by the end of the year, Tamil cinema registered an increase in revenue of nearly 20 per cent. Industry leaders in Bollywood have since been lobbying for such stringent measures on a nation-wide scale to deter video pirates from running loose. This has become all the more imperative since the benefits expected out of shortening release windows are not really trickling in for the film industry. Piracy has not gone up, but it has not come down either. Retailers dealing with counterfeit copies are continuing to do so, especially in small towns, where originals are priced at a premium. The only advantage emerging from an almost simultaneous release of theatrical and video rights is that revenues from both sources can be maximised in the shortest period of time. With international markets fast opening up, this means a massive windfall for the film and video industries.

In the final analysis, what needs to be recognised is that just as theatre could not wish away cinema in the last century, we cannot wish away video in the future. It will have an increasingly dominant role to play in the film business as playing systems become better and screen sizes get larger and there is no loss of picture resolution or sound quality. Film-makers who had devised means to beat the video in the past have now reconciled to its importance in the everyday lives of Indians. We no longer see those fuzzy long shots, cluttered backdrops and strong back-lighting (which would blur out on the small screen) in their films because they have realised

that video has come to stay. The mantra now is to adapt and draw maximum advantage out of it, both creatively and monetarily. Already films made on video have found a degree of legitimacy as several overseas festivals are now being held exclusively for them. At present, they are largely attracting documentary film-makers, but it will not be long before feature-length videos take over. Soon there will also be special categories for video entries in the national film awards announced every year.

These are some of the possibilities waiting to happen. For, what matters ultimately in any business is basic economics. The cost of producing a full-length video feature on Digi Beta, DV Cam or any of the other popular formats in use is inconsequential when compared with what it takes to make a 35 mm production. The handling costs of VCDs/DVDs are just as negligible. Moreover, watching a film on home video with the family is any day less expensive than visiting the theatres. In a price-sensitive market like India, these are factors nobody can afford to overlook. It is only a matter of time before the general public recognises its merits and opts for video as the preferred medium of the future. But then, just as theatre could survive against all odds, cinema will also live ... forever.

four

Riding the Air Waves

After video comes television and radio—cinema's next closest cousins. Let's take radio first, the older of the two. Radio arrived in India as AM, or amplitude modulation, broadcasting in 1923, a good 12 years before All India Radio (AIR) came up. In between, there used to be what were known as 'radio broadcast clubs' run by individuals and associations in their private capacities, more in the nature of leisurely activities than any serious commercial pursuit. The first such radio club was formed in 1927. And exactly half a century later, in 1977, FM (frequency modulation) was launched with its first broadcast service from Madras.

Today, much as AIR officially reaches out to 99 per cent of India's population, it is FM broadcasting, by licensed operators in metros and major towns across the country, which has become the preferred mode of radio reception because of its high quality stereophonic sound. The licensing of radio operators followed a policy decision by the Indian government in 1999 to relax its stranglehold on the broadcast medium and encourage private participation in providing quality radio services across the country. It seemed like a generous gesture then, though soon after, the compulsions became obvious. The popularity of television, and that too of private satellite channels, had virtually crippled AIR. So long as television was in black-and-white and the state-owned Doordarshan (Television India) enjoyed monopoly, there was still some hope for AIR. Vividh Bharati, its highly successful commercial service, raked in the money and kept the habit of listening to the radio alive for most Indians. Its sole selling point, significantly, was a strong film-based content sourced from Bollywood. But when colour television entered the scene with the Delhi Asian Games in 1982, a large section of the radio audience got lured away. During those early days, people who kept the radio on either could not afford television sets or needed it to keep track of time. By the mid-nineties, following the famous 'invasion of the skies' by foreign television channels, a generation of Indians had grown up for whom radio had become redundant. Doordarshan lost its monopoly and AIR was put on life support. Ironically, only private funds have kept these two shining relics of public broadcasting alive.

This brief background places in perspective where Indian broadcasting is headed and how the Hindi film industry can fit into its scheme of things. Once again, as in the case of Bollywood's relations with other media, the equation is one of interdependence. The film industry needs radio, just as radio requires cinema to sustain its content. Today, no radio operator can do without a steady flow of film music, star interviews, off-screen gossip and so on in order to keep listener interest alive. Radio jockeys have become adept at splicing the programmes with clever asides and chatty announcements, not to mention hard news. Information, such as, weather forecasts, currency fluctuations, traffic snarls and water logging in the city is also provided from time to time and can be heard at home or work or on the car stereo while driving. Consequently, FM radio has become an important part of urban living in a very short time. But in all this, the basic hook is cinema—film numbers, particularly yesteryears' hits which are not as easily accessible from the mainstream music market. And for providing this very important resource, Bollywood charges royalties or broadcast fee from radio operators.

Another major benefit Bollywood derives from radio is that it gets an additional platform to advertise its products. Song excerpts and snippets of dialogues from new releases command a tremendous recall value when played repeatedly on radio. In many cases these

plug-ins have heightened curiosity to a point where the listener is prompted to gather additional information on the film from press-ads, publicity hoardings and television spots. Eventually, he buys a cinema ticket. The format adopted now is broadly what Vividh Bharati has been doing for decades; only on FM the messages sound more informal and yet convincing, probably because of the absence of a government tag. It appeals eminently to a generation of young Indians accustomed to multi-tasking and with no time to waste. Radio does not demand 100 per cent attention as the eyes and hands are free to continue with the routine day-to-day activity.

Thus, it should come as no surprise if radio once again figures in the government radar, despite the privatisation of FM channels. The next step, obviously, is to move from a system of bidding for licenses to an even more lucrative and long-lasting mechanism of revenue sharing. The granting of radio licenses had come under fire in May 2000 when the bidding process was opened, leading to major losses to serious players. Since the earnest money for bidding was negligible, several non-serious media groups and speculative bidders entered the fray. This led to a bidding frenzy, resulting in unrealistically high license fee. Radio City Lucknow, Radio Mirchi Pune and Win 94.6 were some of the more prominent FM stations which ran into huge losses and closed down by 2005. Other private players slowly died out. In fact, out of operators in 40 cities that had bid for licenses in May 2000, FM stations in only 12 cities survived for five years and all of them continued to be in the red.

Can there be a way out of this license raj? In most parts of Europe, the Middle East and Africa, radio license fee is paid by households via government levies to help finance public broadcasting. In Germany, by far the largest and most lucrative radio market in Europe, public broadcasters have been demanding an increase in license fee, which is being resisted by private operators. In the U.K., a periodic charter review is required for the renewal of BBC's license, while in The Netherlands, formal rights fee was discontinued in 1999, but the government continues to fund public broadcasting out of general revenues. Elsewhere, in Indonesia, Japan, Malaysia, Pakistan,

Singapore, South Korea and Taiwan, license fee is calculated according to the number of households covered. In New Zealand though, licence fee was eliminated at the end of 1999.

In the U.S., there is satellite radio, which is dominated by two key market players, taking care of over four million subscribers. Satellite radio is a subscription-driven service with signals streaming in directly from satellites and providing every subscriber a choice of up to 100 channels featuring crystal-clear high quality music programmes, interspersed with news, weather reports and sport commentaries. It is said to be the greatest improvement in radio clarity since the advent of FM broadcasting, and it also lends itself to installation in high-end luxury cars at no extra cost to the subscriber. The only drawback, however, is that it lacks local coverage. Thus, in India, World Space could not make much headway with its bouquet of 40 radio channels and installation costs of receivers pegged at a base price of less than Rs 2,000 apiece. The highest it could get to was about 50,000 subscribers in 2005, a figure that has not been able to attract sponsors, Bollywood included.

There is also community radio in India, which began in February 2004 with Anna FM from Anna University, Chennai, on 90.4 MHz FM. The idea behind starting this service was to 'encourage freedom of expression, exchange of information, participation in community development, capacity utilisation in rural areas and the prospering of cultures'. Yet, the most important clause for granting license is that the broadcaster ought to be a government-recognised institution engaged in education, health care, environment protection, agriculture research or rural development. If only cinema were to be included in this list for eligibility in obtaining community radio licenses, the dramatic change that would come about in both the broadcasting sector and the film industry can well be imagined.

As of now, radio holds just about 1 per cent stake in the Indian entertainment industry (as against television commanding the lion's share of 65 per cent). In terms of spot rates also, radio claims a much lower rate (between 2 and 3 per cent) as compared to that of television.

Though this makes the medium more attractive to advertisers, its share of ad-spend continues to be a miserable 2 per cent for several years. The only advertisers drawn to radio are small-time retailers, local estate agents, mobile phone service providers, manufacturers of toilet or floor cleaners and television channel promoters. Even they constitute a reluctant lot, because radio does not provide for the kind of niche programming television is known for. The competition between FM players in the same city is so stiff that nobody wants to take chances in experimenting with content, at least till such time they are constrained to operate within one frequency per city per head.

But then, all is not lost. Sales of radio sets are booming, thanks to a variety of product offerings in the market which are trendy and low-priced. In 2003–2004, many leading manufacturers had slashed the prices of their main models by half and promptly recorded more than double their normal turnover. The Media Research Users Council (MRUC), which conducts a radio audience measurement study (Indian Listenership Track) every year, has predicted an 'explosive growth' in the coming years. Many non-entertainment and non-radio companies are also stepping into the field, both at the national and international levels. For instance, Virgin Radio, which commands a highly successful track record in European radio operations, has been eyeing the Indian market for long. Funnily, a lot of hope is also being pinned on in-car listening (which currently accounts for 20 per cent of radio listening hours among urban Indians) as traffic congestion and snarls in cities get worse.

Tuning In

This broadly gives an idea of the untapped potential radio in India holds which Bollywood can gainfully exploit at an opportune time. As in the past, improvements in broadcast technology will drive the popularity of radio even further. Just as FM with its stereophonic

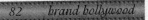
capabilities supplanted AM, the next step ahead would be digital audio broadcasting (DAB) or high definition (HD) radio. HD radio provides near CD-quality sound and also the ability to transmit information on the artiste or the song. Advertisers in the U.S. and Europe are already experimenting with RDS (radio data system) receivers in automobiles. The receivers permit text message displays, otherwise intended to indicate the title of the song being played, name of the artiste, album and other related information. Radio stations are accordingly being equipped with the technology to broadcast commercial text messages to RDS receivers. As automobile manufacturers install RDS equipment in new cars, the potential of this market will expand even further. This is yet another possibility Bollywood could explore in times to come.

The trouble with Bollywood pundits at present is that they are so badly hooked to television that the promise other allied media offer is very often underestimated. Few realise, for instance, that when television viewership drops to rock bottom between 8 am and 12 noon, radio listenership peaks. Quite often consumers imagine they have seen a campaign on television when, in fact, radio was the only advertising medium used. Tests conducted over the years by different media research groups have come up with some similarly astonishing revelations:

1. If 10 per cent of a given television budget is deployed to radio, the efficiency of a campaign increases on an average by 15 per cent.

2. Radio, in isolation, is three-fifths as effective as television in raising advertising awareness at one-seventh the cost.

3. Most effective radio campaigns outperform the average on television. Enjoyment is an important factor but, above all, the best performing ads are well branded.

A good example of how radio and television can come together is the *Indian Idol* talent hunt conducted by Sony TV in 2004–2005. Like many other imported formats on Indian television, it was a

take-off on the *American Idol* show, whereby every Thursday, audiences across the country had to telephonically vote for the most impressive performer of the evening on the programme. Through a process of short-listing and elimination over three months, the participant who polled the maximum number of votes was declared the 'Indian Idol' and awarded a contract of Rs 10 million to cut a song album. But more than that, what took media analysts by surprise was the manner in which the show galvanised the entire nation into taking part in the voting process. For the first time, the common man felt empowered to create a celebrity, and it was this spirit of empowerment which was reinforced by regular radio spots through the weeks as the programme progressed. Before long, even those who did not watch Sony TV got hooked. With witty comments, behind-the-scenes gossip and phone-ins from listeners speculating on the possible winners of every episode, public involvement reached such a feverish pitch that betting syndicates came up in cities like Mumbai and angry mobs took to the streets in small towns every time a 'favorite' contestant lost. Rival television channels and the press could no longer remain silent spectators and unwittingly contributed to the publicity build-up. *Indian Idol* had become a national rage during those three months, and towards its closing episodes, Sony TV was reportedly being hit by an avalanche of as many as 65 million votes after every show. Never before in the history of the Indian entertainment industry had any interactive television programme generated such passion and public frenzy, nationwide.

Of course, many of the votes were the result of multiple calls. According to the show organisers, on an average 15 million votes were identified as 'repeats', leaving Sony with 50 million callers—people who believed that anybody can make it and that by holding centre stage during the selection process, the most deserving candidate would emerge as the 'Indian Idol'. For the channel, the callers were not faceless people. They were individuals with names, families, addresses and telephone numbers, information which made for an invaluable database that Sony got building upon. The moral of the story is that while every other television channel assumes that it knows its consumers, Sony today enjoys the distinction of being the first to be able to actually identify and seek them out at will for their opinion on whatever programme or show it might contemplate in the future. Over time, they will become the real salesmen for the channel.

There are two other important lessons Sony's success story holds for Bollywood. One, in a borderless industry, the lines between film and television, radio and television, film and radio, and so on, are getting increasingly blurred. *Indian Idol* was not the first reality show or talent hunt to be telecast in India; nor is it the last. Regional language channels have been conducting such interactive programmes for several years. Hindi too had its clones (with minor variations in the format), like Channel V's *Pop Stars* (2004–2005) and *Super Singer* (2004–2005), Sahara TV's *Mr & Mrs Bollywood* (2005) and Zee's *India's Best: Cinestars Ki Khoj* (2004–2005), but none of them could match the hype and hoopla of *Indian Idol*, simply because they restricted their promotions to themselves. Sony opened its doors to every other media, including mobile telephony. Even the film industry was roped in with the presence of three prominent Bollywood personalities as judges and the promise of a career in playback singing for the contestants. But the most decisive factor, as many media strategists have pointed out, was the constant drumming in on radio, which the private FM channels provided round the clock.

The second important lesson to be drawn is that audience involvement cannot be taken for granted. A good product alone does not guarantee consumer interest. Unless special efforts are made to identify and then interact with audiences, the whole exercise could be a total waste. Cinema is not an interactive medium like television, but if an effort—no matter what it takes—is made to reach out and seek public participation, the box-office fortunes of a film can change dramatically. A simple SMS inviting suggestions for a title, or a radio appeal for a possible ending to a film should be a good starting point to get the public involved. Whether or not the suggestion gets incorporated by the film-maker is irrelevant; however, public participation is. A cash prize thrown in could serve as an attractive bait. One actor-director released a Tamil film without

a title. That, by itself, was sufficient to arouse public curiosity, and when some prizes were announced for the best suggestions from the audience for a possible title, people trooped into the cinemas in hordes. Film-makers have experimented with such publicity gimmicks on a number of occasions and almost invariably hit pay dirt, all because somehow, somewhere they had managed to touch the audience.

There are a dozen other ways by which Bollywood stands to gain from television, be it as a powerful medium for publicity or for sharing a common pool of talent and infrastructure or as a revenue resource for the content it provides. Likewise, television benefits a great deal from cinema, though the problems here are somewhat peculiar. From contending with the tyranny of cable operators to inconsistent pricing and poor quality of content to outdated technology, price resistance from consumers and a terrible investment climate, television channel owners forever have to grapple with intangibles to keep themselves afloat. Added to these are the odd interventions from government regulatory bodies. And yet, more than 300 channels are beaming over 2,500,000 hours of programming to around 120 million Indian homes round the year. The numbers are only increasing. If this is creating severe capacity constraints, nobody is telling. For, the general objective now is to target the remaining 80 million or 35 per cent of Indian households which do not possess television sets. Since the industry is driven more by subscription than by advertising (on a ratio of 58:42), this will not be easy. But then, everybody is hopeful that market forces will eventually help segment high-paying and low-paying customers and sustain a compounded growth rate of 18 per cent annually for the industry. Besides, once cable networks turn digital, more channels can be accommodated and make market penetration easier.

The prevailing environment of optimism has resulted in the launch of 15 to 20 new television channels, on an average, every year, particularly on news, lifestyle, business, spiritual and kids' programmes, subjects which, till a few years back, were considered uninteresting and less lucrative than the traditional family soap operas. The latter

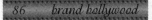

continues to dominate viewership ratings and attracts the highest ad premiums. Yet, instead of developing on these segments, mainline channels like Zee, Star and MTV have begun venturing into newer areas, including the regional markets. The latest, though, is the 'crossover craze', a cue taken from the Hindi film industry, whereby music channels are launching soaps, news channels are venturing into lifestyle shows and business channels are foraying into spiritual discourses.

◼ Niche Channels

Surely there has to be some method in this madness. One indicator is that television is increasingly entering the bedrooms of Indian households which can afford more than one TV set for the family. So while programmes of common interest (like soaps and movies) are usually watched on the set in the drawing room, the grandmother might like exclusive access to a spiritual channel in her room, and in the kid's room, Cartoon Network could be on. Effectively, niche channels are finding acceptability like never before. Many, in fact, feel that family viewing of programmes will soon become a thing of the past as television sets are fast moving out of the living room to other rooms in urban households. Even the bathroom is proving to be a good enough place for a set. At times, the same programme could be playing simultaneously in different rooms on different sets. In effect, like the dining table, the television set is losing its primacy as the focal point of family get-togethers and bonding in Indian homes.

The other key indicator is that regardless of what may be said of a consumerist economy, the viewer has no real choice over what he watches. He remains completely at the mercy of the local cable guy for whatever is doled out. Till such time as DTH (direct to home) or IP-TV (Internet Protocol Television) comes in full on a scale, the last mile environment will continue to be monopolised by the local

cable operator, leaving little choice to the viewer. The former is notorious for arm-twisting his way into charging whatever he pleases from subscribers, not allowing another operator into his turf, under-declaring subscriptions and resisting technology by way of alternative viewing platforms. Ideally, broadcasters need to look at partnering solutions for the last mile so as to create a level playing field. Instead, they have left these issues for government regulatory bodies to deal with and are focusing on launching new channels in the belief that catering differentially to varying segments of the population will be beneficial in the long run. There is some basis in this belief because mass entertainment channels have already ceded viewership to the many niche channels that are coming up. The front-runners in this area are as follows:

News Channels

Current affairs and business channels have registered a consistent 100 per cent growth in viewership annually for several years now. In 2001, from two dominant news channels, one major business channel and two international English news channels, this segment had burgeoned into 11 mainstream news channels and a slew of regional channels in 2005, together generating revenues of more than Rs 5 billion annually. The reasons for this are obvious. Tabloid news formats with chatty reporting, focus on crime stories and sensationalism and sound bytes from the scene of action have come as welcome diversions from the staid and officious coverage Doordarshan was known for. Production values have also gone up admirably with snazzy studio props, high profile news anchors and participation of celebrity guests. In order to keep the eyeballs glued to the screen, film content from Bollywood now accounts for an estimated 20 per cent of airtime on news channels across the board. Small wonder, large corporate houses are eyeing this niche, giving news and current affairs reporting a further boost.

Children's Channels

Advertisers of school stationery, kids' clothes, games and toys as well as consumer durables are cashing in on the 'pester power' of

children, thereby pushing this segment to unprecedented heights of growth. The earliest to make their presence in the children's space were the three international majors—Cartoon Network, Nickleodeon and Walt Disney Productions. Then Indian broadcasters got into the act, beginning with Zee and followed by content providers like Pentamedia and UTV. Now more than a dozen players have entered the space and domestic broadcasters are particularly well placed in filling the current void of localised programming. They are taking their cue from mature television economies where locally generated children's programmes have proved to be the strongest growth engines for such channels. Besides, international channels which have all along been dishing out dubbed, multilingual programmes are looking at original Indian material for inclusion in their programme menu. The depth of programming, coupled with expansion of advertising space, have consequently taken children's channels on the track of accelerated progress.

Regional Channels

For more than a decade, television channels in Maharashtra, West Bengal and the four southern states of Tamil Nadu, Andhra Pradesh, Karnataka and Kerala have been jostling for viewers' attention amidst a mass of mainline Hindi (and English) channels. Now those regional channels are coming into their own. It is not as though viewership within (or even outside) their respective states was lacking, but in the face of fierce competition between channels and the absence of advertising support, regional players had almost lost out. Over time though, all their ills, including low production budgets, copycat programming and, most importantly, low ad rate realisations, have been reversed. They have become more targeted and segmented in their approach, thereby raising their ads-to-viewership ratio to almost that of the English films and some prime entertainment channels. In other words, regional channels can now command a relative premium on a proportionately low viewership base, as opposed to mass channels. But a lot of ground still remains to be covered.

Sports Channels

Cricket mania is the prime reason for bolstering the growth of sports channels in India. Since the World Cup in 2003 (when India ended runners-up), followed by the Australian and Pakistan tours, cricket viewership has been on a consistent upswing. Consequently, telecast rights for key matches are costing sports channels phenomenal amounts, but they are all willing to pay (some even landing up in court to contest decisions in favour of rivals) to stay ahead in the race. For instance, while the telecast rights for the Australia–New Zealand World Cup in 1992 fetched U.S.$ 10 million, the rights for the 2003 World Cup in South Africa fetched U.S.$ 85 million—a giant leap of 750 per cent in 12 years. In comparison, the telecast rights for the Olympic Games went up from U.S.$ 350 million (Atlanta 1984) to U.S.$ 1.5 billion (Athens 2004)—an increase of just over 300 per cent in 20 years. As for other sports, viewer response is comparatively negligible. Nevertheless, sports channels have been trying to generate interest in non-cricketing events by providing slots for soccer, hockey, basketball, tennis and Formula 1 racing and have succeeded to a major extent. The exploits of Sania Mirza in tennis or Narain Karthikeyan in Formula 1 are being as keenly followed as Mahendra Singh Dhoni's batting scores and Irfan Pathan's wicket hauls.

Apart from basic foresight, there are some strong economic compulsions for the launch of these niche channels. One, an increase in the number of mass entertainment channels with a surfeit of 'me too' content had led to a fragmentation of viewership patterns. Two, advertisers now enjoy the option to reach out to a focused target group at a fraction of their earlier costs. And three, too many high profile shows, particularly family dramas, interactive programmes, daily soaps, talent contests and adult programming have collapsed in recent years, notwithstanding the media hype, high star value and millions of rupees invested in their development. They have had to either be thematically re-oriented or yanked off the air.

Furthermore, as audiences get exposed to international channels, their expectations go up and they discriminate on the quality and treatment of content. Spiritual channels and healthcare channels, which started on a shaky note, are now looking spruced up with top quality production values and robust advertising streams. Even city-centric channels, known for their sloppy coverage of building collapses, road accidents and crime stories, have fallen in line and are earning the loyalty of viewers. But overall, it would appear that Indian television is still dominated by mass entertainment and regional channels, splitting a market share of 80 per cent equally between them. If we were to keep these two genres out, the remaining 20 per cent is shared between Hindi film channels (8 per cent), news channels (4 per cent), sports channels (3 per cent), English entertainment channels (2 per cent) and other sundry channels (3 per cent).

From time to time, these percentages would shift a few notches up or down, but broadly they are indicative of the viewership pattern on an all-India level. Regional variations can well be expected, just as an event of national importance like the general elections, natural disasters (say, the Gujarat earthquake or the tsunami catastrophe in southern India) or even an Indo-Pakistan cricket series could temporarily alter the viewership pattern. For the purposes of a long-term media strategy though, the national-level percentage break-up holds good. Two other related factors of consequence, especially when planning the release of a film for telecast, are the programme clutter during prime time and a swell in the number of hour-long programmes during weekends.

Digital Migration

While these may be seen both as challenges and opportunities, certain grey areas within the television industry cannot be over-looked. For instance, despite the prevailing boom, independent

television production houses were not able to grow as expected and had to perforce either shut down or move into allied businesses. There are a few exceptions who have managed to consolidate their position and corner the market of sitcoms and soaps. In order to break their monopoly, either television channels will have to develop a higher proportion of in-house content, or more production houses should be stepping in and integrating their business models with those of the broadcasters. Furthermore, adaptation of existing content to digital and other delivery platforms is a worrisome factor. We are still at a stage where much of television software is generated on analogue platforms. Not only has this to be converted into digital formats, it has also to be fine-tuned to suit the delivery platforms of each individual format, such as, HDTV or IP-TV. Only then will Indian television be able to advance to the next stage of its evolution and keep pace with the developments elsewhere in the world. Here, a brief overview of key international trends would be in order.

In large parts of the Asia-Pacific region, Latin America and Canada, multi-channel households (or viewers having access to television via cable, satellite, digital and other means) are driving the television distribution markets. However, in the developed world, such as, Europe and the Middle East, growth is tardy because the number of these households has reached saturation point. Subscribers are migrating to higher-priced premium services. Spending on pay-per-view and video-on-demand is thus rapidly growing, though, in the long run, with shorter release windows for movies, they do not have much of a future. As for piracy of cable signals, markets of Asia-Pacific and Latin America are the worst hit.

In the U.S., multi-channel household penetration is close to 90 per cent, leaving little room for overall subscriber growth. This has compelled cable and DBS (direct broadcast satellite) providers to cut costs and consolidate their holdings. In 2003, Comcast Corp acquired AT&T Corp's cable holdings (consisting primarily of Media One and Telecommunications Inc). Thereafter, EchoStar tried to acquire

DIRECTV, but the U.S. Federal Communications Commission disallowed the deal, thereby prompting DBS providers to look at vertical mergers. News Corp was eventually granted permission to acquire DIRECTV. Significantly, the DBS service is priced lower than that of cable and it typically subsidises or provides the receiving dish for free. It has become even more competitive with the added advantage of HDTV services and local stations gaining entry into newer markets.

In order to counter the popularity of DBS, cable operators are entering into joint ventures with telephone companies to provide wireless telephony. Till 2003, many American states did not permit telephone companies to extend their lines long-distance and as such they were in no position to provide television services. In 2004, when this embargo was lifted, the carriers combined long-distance telephony with DSL (digital service line) broadband Internet access. The next step was to enter the television distribution market and huge sums were spent on fibre deployments. Effectively, subscribers are being offered local and long-distance telephone services bundled with standard television and broadband Internet access. Mounting competition and improvements in communications technology have also enabled low-cost voice-over IP (VoIP) and a host of other services:

Digital Video Recording (DVR)

Ever since Time Warner came up with DVR in the U.S., technology has advanced to a point where a viewer is able to watch a programme already in progress from the very beginning by what is known as the 'start over' facility. This facility uses DVR functionality but does not permit commercial skipping.

Video-on-Demand (VoD)

Cable operators are allocating more channel space to VoD in order to emphasise their advantage over DBS. Typically, subscribers are able to access a library of 200-odd titles through this facility, absolutely free of cost, thanks to tie-ups with some leading film production houses.

Pay-Per-View

This is a service available in virtually all multi-channel households whereas VoD is essentially limited to digital cable. Internet distribution though, is also emerging. As cable operators start shifting from pay-per-view to VoD, growth in this segment will correspondingly slow down.

Interconnects

As a vital marketing tool, interconnects enable advertisers to book time on all cable systems in the market with a single buy. With interconnects turning more sophisticated, buying, placing and inserting ads through the cable system have become very convenient. The next step is to provide different versions of the same ad to different neighbourhoods, a feature not available with most television stations.

It is now only a matter of time before all these facilities will be available in India and a similar scenario will prevail here also. For all those engaged in the promotion of Bollywood films, this is a huge marketing opportunity. The minor reasons for holding it back are the delays in firming up a regulatory mechanism and exceedingly slow digital upgrades. The transition from analogue to digital networks is a long process. The operators will have to simulcast channels in analogue and digital modes, and in the interim, additional bandwidth is required to make space for both sets of channels. Moreover, subscribers will need to invest in set-top boxes or digital receivers. Alternatively, expensive digital television sets would have to be bought (actually, imported) which have the capabilities inbuilt. But then, digitisation is inevitable. It will create greater bandwidth space and more advertising platforms, not to mention superior picture, sound quality and scope for newer value-added services, such as, triple play (voice, video and data), multi-view and electronic programme guides. Above all, it will enable film producers to choose between either carpet-bombing the marketplace or concentrate on precision targeting the audience through niche channels. The mushrooming of newer channels will further iron out the anomalies the television industry and film trade are faced with. The measures

initiated by some Asian countries in this direction would be enlightening:

China

In view of the Beijing Summer Olympics, China Central Television launched the nation's first digital service in September 2004. Four months later, in January 2005, Shanghai Interactive Television introduced the second digital service. The State Administration for Radio, Film and Television arranged for banks to provide cable operators with loans at low interest rates to subsidise set-top boxes and, in certain exceptional cases, even provided free set-top boxes to accelerate the transition from analogue to digital. The drive is reminiscent of the Indian government's efforts in 1982, when the Delhi Asian Games set the deadline for television to make the switch from black-and-white to the colour mode. The target for full digital conversion in China is 2015.

Japan

The Japanese ministry of internal affairs and communications has set 2010 as the time frame for national digitisation of television. Already, the market has access to a digital communications satellite (since 1996) and a digital broadcast satellite (from 2000) for digital cable trials. 2011 is the target for full digitisation of terrestrial services. The moment digital coverage reaches the level of analogue and the take-up rate hits 85 per cent (including reception over cable systems), analogue transmission will be switched off. Progress in this regard is being monitored every three years, area by area.

Taiwan

The National Information Infrastructure under the Executive Yuan has set January 2008 as the deadline to effect a 'complete digital migration' for the Taiwan broadcasting industry. Since both digital cable and terrestrial penetration are low, the Government Information Office awarded a digital cable television license to telecom giant, CHT, enabling it to launch digital services in Taipei City and Northern Taiwan. However, its operations are being monitored and

regulated by the many restrictions applicable to cable operators. Meanwhile, the Executive Yuan is drafting a new statute to boost the island's digitisation plans on television for the future.

South Korea

The Korean government has adopted a two-pronged approach towards 'total digital transition' by focusing on (*i*) broadcasting-related networks and (*ii*) information-and-communication networks. Television falls under the former, for which the building of a national infrastructure should be completed by 2010. Cable television operators and service providers have been urged to convert to digital broadcasting technologies before 2008. By then, it is estimated that six to nine million subscribers would have made the transition from the analogue mode, thereby implying a 50 to 70 per cent conversion rate.

Hong Kong

Terrestrial broadcasters in Hong Kong are already under pressure to begin simulcast broadcasting on both analogue and digital modes by 2007 (at the latest) and to extend the coverage of their digital networks to 75 per cent of the subscriber base by 2008. In another five years (or 2012) the government proposes to switch off analogue broadcasting, though 'subject to further market and technical studies'. The costs for this digital transmission upgrade are being indirectly borne by the government, as it has abolished the 10 per cent royalty it used to charge on the advertising revenues from terrestrial television.

India can well pick up some valuable cues from these initiatives, only that, given its size and political culture, the transition will take much longer than any of these countries. By 2010—when China will be past the halfway mark towards 100 per cent digitisation—it is estimated that barely 18 per cent or 13 million Indian households will be accessing digital platforms. Digital subscriber off-take is expected to be more rapid in metros, while the roll-out will be slower in other cities, towns and rural areas. There Doordarshan's low-priced

DTH services will continue to command a larger market share than that of private operators. IP-TV and broadband over copper will also be restricted to major cities (given the high per-line investment required), and the price wars between existing cable operators will become more intense. Of course, a lot of this could change depending upon the regulatory environment and whether new players like established telecom companies feel tempted enough to pitch in. In that case, the market share of digital platforms will go up significantly.

As for programme content, a majority of subscribers (regardless of the platform they are on) can be expected to opt for a package that fulfils the basic ingredients of infotainment. 'Light viewers', or those who watch television for less than 20 hours in a week, will be the most dominant segment of viewership with no particular loyalty to a channel or genre. In the face of an onslaught of channels and competing platforms, the behaviour of this segment will be closely monitored by broadcasters, as it would have a direct bearing on their pricing and subscriber off-take. For Bollywood producers and distributors, these are the very eyeballs that need to be arrested through attractive packaging of promotion material and innovative marketing strategies.

five

Battle of the Screens

If television is the most dominant of the Indian media, live entertainment has been the fastest developing. Since 2002, the event management and stage shows sector has maintained a steady growth of 20 to 25 per cent annually, largely because of its integration with the film and television businesses. Today, no film awards' function is held without the association of an event management company, and no star-studded event is ever missed by television. Whether they are annual awards' functions like Filmfare or Screen in Mumbai, or the International Film Festival of India in Goa, or a Bollywood charity show anywhere on the globe, event management companies get into their act, with television channels following right behind them. Even for such overseas shows as the Zee Telefilm and IIFA (International Indian Film Academy) awards' functions, professionals from India are flown over to set the stage and the works. The revenue from bidding for exclusive telecast rights for such extravaganzas may not be at the level of what a cricket match generates, but it is fast getting there.

Indian television desperately needs film content to grab the viewers' eyes and, in turn, ad revenues. The role of event management companies is to package the shows in as attractive a manner as possible, not so much for the live audience, but for the benefit of television cameras. The formatting of the shows is also cleverly tailored to meet the requirements of television, replete with interruptions for commercial breaks and so on, much as they might appear to be beamed live.

Every single act of the show is worked out with extreme precision by the event management company in advance. At times, the telecast is deliberately delayed by a few hours or days after the event has taken place, mainly to catch a prime-time slot or weekend viewership. The point, though, is that the integration of films, television and live entertainment has become so complete that a charity show, *Help! Telethon Concert 2005*, held one Sunday afternoon for the 2004-tsunami victims in Tamil Nadu, proved a phenomenal success. A joint initiative of the Film and Television Guild of India, some leading event management companies and TV channels like Doordarshan, Star, Zee, Sab, Sony Entertainment and Zoom, the six-hour stage show on 6 February 2005 featuring film stars in Mumbai was concurrently telecast by all channels across the country, thereby opening multiple revenue streams, both from ticket sales and airtime bookings—all of which were channelised for the rehabilitation of tsunami victims. The simulcast was the biggest ever fundraiser held in Asia.

Another example of how television has become dependent on live entertainment and vice versa was provided by the reality show, *Sa Re Ga Ma Pa*, on Zee TV in 2005–2006. The format demanded that finalists interact live with sections of the public in various cities like Kolkata, Guwahati, Lucknow and Delhi. At these venues, sets were erected with elaborate lighting and sound systems, turning these side shows into mega 'talk of the town' events. For the contestants, organisers, the television channel, sponsors and, of course, the event management companies, the major hype that was generated translated into more phone-ins and SMSs in support of the contestants. The success of this strategy made media pundits sit up and take notice. They realised that when it came to reaching out to specific audience groups during shows, the impact of live entertainment events can be far more effective than traditional promotions, such as, outdoor publicity and other in-programming devices. The potential of this medium, however, remains to be exploited by Bollywood producers.

The other touch points in this business are as follows:

Guaranteed Ticket Sales

Event management companies not only organise shows but are also able to guarantee ticket sales and raise funds needed to cover costs. The popularity of Bollywood 'star nites' round the year in different parts of the globe is proof of this. So lucrative has this line of business become that most stars are earning more from stage shows than films and are virtually globe-trotting for the best part of the year. At another level, they have raised awareness about Bollywood cinema worldwide, prompting international pop singers and bands like Rolling Stones, Bryan Adams, Sting and Shaggy to perform in India. These shows are so well organised that they are never known to run into losses due to absence of audience support.

Domestic Events

Indian festivals are getting a fair share of live coverage because of the side shows held by entertainment companies, whether it is at the annual Goa Carnival, the Pushkar Cattle Fair, the Desert Festival at Jaisalmer or the Khajuraho Dance Festival. In this respect, event management companies have become promoters of Indian culture. Television channels, which would otherwise show scant interest in routine calendar events, fairs and festivals, are now vying for telecast rights to cover these entertaining shows. Likewise, localised sporting events, such as, the Mumbai Marathon and the Punjab Rural Olympics, are finding viewership across the regional divide, thanks to the imaginative packaging by event management companies.

Personal Events

Rising income levels have led to ostentatious celebrations of family and personal events, like weddings and birthdays, by the nation's nouveau riche. The family weddings of certain diamond merchants, leading industrialists and media celebrities, organised entirely by professional event management companies, are indicative of the times to come. From booking of hotel rooms and transport for the guests to basic details like fixing the menu, flower arrangements, getting hold of a pundit, the fireworks' display and so on, everything is taken care of by professionals. Even getting film stars to dance and entertain guests for a price is arranged by them. As many as 20 Indian celebrity weddings take place on an average (both within the country and overseas) every year, generating a revenue upwards of Rs 3 billion annually for the event management sector.

Star Participation

No longer satisfied with performing on stage, Bollywood stars are now getting actively involved in organising live shows across the globe. Almost every top male star has floated an event management company either in his own name or by proxy. All of them are heavily booked several months in advance, primarily because of the high trust value they command with their overseas associates who, in turn, can be assured of a high profile star participation. Television channels too find them more reliable than the old players who have graduated into the business from small-time wedding decorators and suppliers of fireworks. When a superstar organises a show, no colleague in the film industry lets him down and the chances of last-minute dropouts are minimal. So within the acting fraternity, everybody is making merry while the old timers have been relegated to the sidelines, holding less-profitable shows within the country.

While these are positive indicators for the live entertainment sector, on the negative side, concerns of unprofessional dealings, racketeering and fly-by-night operators persist. Barely a dozen players, each with average revenues of Rs 200 million annually, hold a semblance of goodwill. The rest, comprising 70 per cent of the industry, are completely unorganised. They are small-time players, operating out of mofussil towns and holding parallel lines of business. For them, organising cultural events (theatre festivals, music concerts and dance recitals), felicitations, contests and ramp shows are one-off engagements for which the charges are a tiny fraction of what the big daddies in the business have been claiming. Yet, the billings from this unorganised segment, cumulatively, make for three to four times the gross turnover of the organised sector.

Another cause for concern is the lack of infrastructure for hosting events on a grand scale. Metros like Mumbai, Delhi and Bangalore

can boast of the best infrastructural facilities in the world but are severely handicapped by a space crunch, especially during the monsoon months. Cities which have the space suffer from logistic problems. Either way, it is a no-go situation and compromises have to be made one way or the other. Of late though, some hospitality giants have been pushing their resorts, banquet halls and palaces as 'the most desirable venues', but again, the infrastructure is lacking. Sports complexes and exhibition grounds in satellite towns are turning out to be a more attractive proposition, even as basic facilities might have to be created from scratch. The budgets involved in holding some mega events are often so huge that they can easily absorb the costs of permanently upgrading the available infrastructure, which is otherwise lying neglected.

This brings us to the third and final problem area. In any Indian city, holding a live event requires 13 to 18 permissions from the government and civic bodies—the police have to give their clearance for the use of loud speakers and traffic disruptions; the fire brigade must make its own assessment of basic safety norms; the customs department needs to give its approval for all imported equipment; and so on. All this takes time and leads to endless hardship and harassment for the event organisers unless palms are greased. The only way out is to operate a system of single window clearance, as is prevalent in the West. The irony of the situation is that in India, the government in its overall scheme of things considers live entertainment a corrupting and avoidable luxury on the one hand, and a very important milch cow for the huge tax revenues it yields on the other hand. In fact, the rules are so punishing that entertainment tax for live events in some states has to be paid prior to the sale of tickets and the relevant authority is supposed to stamp each ticket as 'tax paid'. This means that if there are any unsold tickets, the amount of tax paid is a loss for the event managers. The only way to duck this requirement is to host un-ticketed shows and collect money in the guise of donations or donor passes. But then, there are a host of other taxes like income tax, service tax and so on, from which there can be no escape.

▮ Personal Computers

Next in the line of media options is the monitor of your personal computer. After video and television, this is the most important screen every movie producer should be targeting. The reason they are not doing so is that PC penetration is abysmally low in India as compared to the developed world. But the rate at which computer literacy is spreading, it should not be long before we catch up with the West. Aiding this process are factors, such as, revenue opportunities emerging from the digital delivery of content and rapidly declining prices of computer hardware and peripherals. Already many households in urban India can claim to possess more than one PC for the family, each with an allotted function or user. The husband could be using one for the work he carries home from office while the wife could be sharing another PC with her teenage daughter to maintain household accounts, surfing the Net and keeping in touch with friends and relations through e-mail. For the son, there could be yet another PC on which he could do his school projects and play computer games. Depending on their function, manufacturers are now working towards creating high-performance super-specialised PC platforms for what they call 'Indian digital homes' of the future:

Creativity PC

This is an all-purpose platform that provides for the creation of rich digital content and handling of daily productivity tasks while also serving as the central content acquisition and storage system in a digital home network. It has the ability to multi-task while the user is importing, storing, editing, creating and distributing digital content—both audio and visual. It can also encode and trans-code video for remote consumption while supporting local activities, such as, Internet browsing and gaming. When equipped with a television tuner, the Creativity PC can capture HD (high definition) and SD (standard definition) content and distribute it across the network.

Entertainment PC

This is an easy-to-use consumer electronics device that enables the entire family to enjoy premium or personal digital content, including games, stereo and the home theatre menu. Typically, its location is in the front hall or family room, whereby applications are optimised for viewing at a 10 feet distance and controlled using a hand-held remote or game-pad controller. The Entertainment PC has a form factor that presents a sleek appearance and minimises operational noise to deliver an optimal entertainment experience. It can also be equipped with a television tuner for content distribution. But it differs from other key platforms in that it is not intended for editing or creating new personal content.

Lifestyle PC

It delivers a combination of digital home experiences on to a single platform—both the traditional two feet experience of productivity and communications as well as the 10 feet experience characterised by the local enjoyment of digital content through the use of remote control. Lifestyle PCs come in different shapes and sizes—ranging from typical desktops to mini towers to the small form factor and all-in-one designs—depending on the user's requirements and availability of physical space. Like any other PC, it can also be equipped with a television tuner to capture SD and HD content. Its quiet and unobtrusive functioning makes it ideal for constrained spaces such as a bedroom, hotel suite, one room apartment, or dormitory.

Extreme Gaming PC

For ardent gaming and technology enthusiasts, this is the most definitive digital home platform that affords a combination of high performance, expandability and customised flexibility. With its large, expandable chassis to enable end-user upgrading (at the time of purchase or later) and a 'no compromise' approach, the Extreme Gaming PC is designed to deliver the ultimate gaming experience. It has a large cache size and employs cutting-edge technologies for robust artificial intelligence, fast game loads, smooth frame rates

and realistic simulation of physical worlds. Typically, its location is a home office or the children's room.

Home Mobility PC

It allows users to create and enjoy content in a mobile form factor, combining a full-featured PC experience with the flexibility to move from one room to another or for the occasional use outside the home. The Home Mobility PC is a typical mainstream laptop, which supports content creation, productivity tasks and media consumption. Premium content can be acquired over the Internet on a home media server, such as, Entertainment PC or Creativity PC. It also allows content consumption and acquisition anywhere in the home, thereby enabling the user to bring the PC and entertainment experience to more communal areas, such as, the kitchen or living room.

Mobile Entertainment PC

This platform is optimised for recreation and enjoyment, such as, watching movies or television programmes, sharing and editing photographs and playing games anywhere in the house. It also allows for a rich media and communications experience with added PC functionality in a portable all-in-one factor, thus enabling the user to carry the entertainment experience wherever he pleases. The PC has a large screen (17 inches or more) and in-built features like a camera and high definition audio. It includes an integrated television tuner or, instead, provides access to a tuner in another platform in the house. The embedded camera and voice over IP (VoIP) technology support a rich spectrum of communications capabilities, such as, video calls and virtual gatherings with friends and family far away. It also supports features like a media stack, Bluetooth wireless technology, remote control and array microphones which make it the most convenient multipurpose computer-media-communications device ever created.

On-the-Go PC

It provides highly mobile users with a sleek, light (15 inches or smaller) and supremely efficient system, having optimised battery

life for use in and out of the home. The On-the-Go PC supports content creation, productivity tasks, media consumption and can easily be synchronised with a home network to download content, such as, family or holiday photographs, television programmes and movies for viewing outside the home.

Now, let us see how these systems would function in a typical Indian digital home. Say, the Kapoors in Delhi have just installed a Creativity PC in the family study. When they purchased the PC, they opted for the additional dual television tuner to serve as a central personal video recorder for everybody in the household to access. On a Sunday morning, Mr Kapoor uses the Creativity PC to keep tabs on work projects and e-mails, and while he is working, the PC can work in the background to trans-code compressed data over a broadband connection. In the afternoon, Mrs Kapoor uses this powerful system to edit vacation photographs and encode digital videos before adding them to the family's website. She works with the assurance that the PC's anti-virus and firewall programmes are running continuously to protect the network, without compromising the performance she needs. For, at that moment, her daughters are in their bedroom watching a sitcom, the programme having been recorded earlier on the Entertainment PC, which is streaming the content to their room using a digital media adapter. Meanwhile, the Entertainment PC is being used by their father and brother to check out the hundreds of hours of recorded and imported video in addition to the family's growing library of digital music. By the evening, when everybody congregates at the dining table, Mr Kapoor will use the small factor version of a Lifestyle PC with a flat panel display and remote control to catch up with the day's news and Mrs Kapoor will be accessing recipe information in a second window. Next year, when their elder daughter heads for medical college, she will be taking with her a full-size desktop version of the Lifestyle PC which will be able to handle her most demanding course work as well as serve as a personal video recorder for both standard and high definition content. Not to be left out, the other sister has demanded the Mobile Entertainment PC while the brother is hung up on a Gaming PC for his next birthday. He is aware of not only the latest 3-D action games, but also ways to configure a system for high-speed networking. Recently, his friend swapped his stock PC box for a clear plastic case with neon illumination and a high performance cooling system.

Given this scenario, the business opportunities available to Bollywood film-makers can well be imagined. The only obstacle in their path for digital delivery and distribution of movies is what may be called the 'compatibility factor'. These are still early days to expect standardisation of equipment among PC manufacturers. So, it is possible that while a remote (the mouse is getting gradually extinct) may work on one PC, another of a different make may not. Synchronisation between all PCs in a so-called digital environment will become all the more difficult, unless they are bought at the same time from the same manufacturer. Or, all the manufacturers, along with telecom companies and service providers, will have to sit together and agree upon some common acceptable standards for all equipment and peripherals. Such matchmaking involves cross-industry collaboration, something that is inconceivable at this stage of technology evolution and cut-throat competition.

Content protection and rights management are other problem areas which will bother both film producers and service providers in the future. As of now, the technology for streaming visual and audio content from one PC platform to another is available, but what happens when a neighbour, by virtue of his proximity and equipped with a compatible system, has access to the same network? In the absence of fool-proof DTCP (digital transmission content protection), premium content could become public property. The revenue opportunity arising out of digital distribution gets immediately diluted thus. In fact, this has become such a problem in China that many households are discontinuing subscriptions with cable operators and refraining from installing anything beyond a utility PC. Yet, a market survey conducted in some multi-PC households in that country in March 2005 revealed that the consumer is not really dishonest. Among families known to download four to five movies a month from the Internet, 37 per cent were willing to pay (because of superior picture and sound quality), 26 per cent were

not sure and 47 per cent were not willing. The reason cited by the last section was simple: Why should they pay when others are enjoying the same benefits for free? Essentially, they are pleading for instituting a non-discriminatory mechanism whereby everybody gets what he or she pays for. And this, by implication, means the intervention of a government regulatory body.

Animation and Gaming

India's creative skills in the field of animation films have been universally applauded. From the day Dadasaheb Phalke made his stop-motion short film on matchsticks and coins in 1914 to a time when foreign feature film producers are seeking inputs from Indian animators, the growth of the animation industry has been phenomenal—but in fits and starts. It was as late as in 2002 that 3-D animation production work for feature films began to be outsourced to India. Till then, much of the work carried out in the country was in 2-D, meant either for the Cartoon Film Unit of the state-run Films Division or for the advertising industry. Senior artists like Ram Mohan and Bhim Sain have spearheaded the growth of the Indian animation industry for many years since Independence. The future now rests on the talent emerging from the film institutes in Pune and Kolkata and, more significantly, on the National Institute of Design (NID) in Ahmedabad.

As computer generated images take over freehand drawings, artists and illustrators have become anonymous entities. They all are now supposed to be animators. In fact, overseas producers regard animators as computer geeks and the business handled by Indians is technically classified as 'software outsourcing'—just like any other IT-enabled BPO (business process outsourcing). But no matter how they may be described, the fact is that Indians are handling as many as 15-odd projects for overseas producers at any given time and, by virtue of their innovative skills and creativity, have taken the industry to a position of pre-eminence in the field of animated

cinematography. Some of the better known animation works handled by Indians in recent times include the BBC series *Tales of Jack Frost* (2004), Animation Bridge's *The Three Amigos* (2003), Telly Awards winner *Kids' Ten Commandments* (2003) and Cine Golden Eagle award winner *Wemmicks: A Most Wonderful Gift* (2004). Digital visual effects have been created for Hindi films like *Murder* (2004), *Krishna Cottage* (2004), *Shaadi Ka Laddoo* (2004), *Hum Tum* (2004) as well as *Chura Liya Hai Tumne* (2003) while, within the television arena, animation work deserving mention are *Sonapuri* (2003), *Gharwali Uparwali Aur Sunny* (2004), *Shararat* (2002) and *Karishma Ka Karishma* (2003). There are some notable examples of clay-mated commercials as well, such as the one for a national bank (with Chinta Mani as the key character) and another for a reputed car battery brand.

Oddly enough, for all the expertise, no full-fledged 3-D animated movie has yet been produced in India with Indian capital. (V.G. Sampat's 100-minute feature in 2005 on the monkey god, *Hanuman*, was a 2-D film.) A 3-D animation film costs at least seven times more to mount than a normal live action feature. Low demand for original content, coupled with huge investments on infrastructure and manpower have rendered such ventures economically non-viable in Indian conditions. But when these very costs are compared to those prevailing internationally, India holds a competitive edge over other countries. In 2005, the cost of production of a half-hour animated programme in the U.S. was between $250,000 and $400,000. The same material and footage in South Korea had cost $150,000 and $110,000 in Taiwan. But in India, it was possible to get an identical work of the same duration done for approximately $60,000. Taking into account the low cost of labour and infrastructure, plus the fact that computer-based animation offers between 30 and 40 per cent cost reduction over traditional, manually generated animated films, the overall saving to the overseas producer makes India a very attractive destination for animation work.

China is a strong rival in this area because of a similarly large pool of low-cost skilled manpower mostly engaged in developing content

for local consumption. It has been losing out to us solely because it cannot match the command over English which Indians possess. Somehow, for film producers in the West, language seems to be a key factor in doing business. The Chinese understand this and are accordingly seeking a competitive advantage out of aggressively marketing themselves globally, and, with the support of their government (in terms of finance and infrastructure), they have made some huge dents in India's business. The Japanese are also very much organised in their pursuit of overseas animation projects and, for many years, have been sponsoring visits of studio executives from the U.S. to their country. India faces intense competition from the Filipinos, Koreans and Taiwanese as well. Despite charging a premium for their services, they are being sought after by quality-conscious producers in the U.S. and Europe. Their work is supposed to be far more sophisticated and refined than what Indian companies are known to offer.

Now, all these competitors are growing in strength with every passing day, simply because they happen to enjoy the support, financial and otherwise, from their respective governments, something Indian animators do not and cannot even dream of. In comparison to the studios in Japan, South Korea, China or even the Philippines, the facilities in India are very basic and rudimentary. An animation studio to match the standards of, say, Pixar or Blue Sky, is almost impossible to set up with private capital anywhere. The Indian government understands this but has refrained from taking any action because the industry is largely disorganised and lacks a single unified body to represent its interests. All it has for a saviour is the NASSCOM (National Association of Software and Service Companies), which, in any case, is so over-burdened with issues directly related to the telecom and IT sectors that it has little time to spare for animators. Consequently, the latter are left to their devices and have had to make do with low-end work, mostly on 2-D (rather than 3-D), to remain afloat.

Significantly, during the mid-nineties, when animation work was first being outsourced to India, the then players tried to grab as

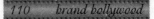

much business as possible and, in fact, made a killing, but at the expense of quality. This adversely affected the reputation of Indian animation studios, and producers found it hard to justify high quality work at low costs. To complicate matters, errors in estimation crept in, largely because of a complex system of accounting for a diverse set of artistic disciplines, such as, lighting, camera and effects, which are then integrated into a technological process. And when other countries with superior technology stepped in, raising industry standards, Indian animators were completely on the back foot. The only way they could fight back to regain their position was by building on their strong resource base of trained manpower. Institutions like NID and WEBEL (a joint venture by the West Bengal government and a private company) began turning out professionals skilled in multi-media software, such as, Maya, 3D Studio Max, Gif Animator, Flash and Tictactoon. These efforts have finally borne fruit as Indian animators are now able to bid for higher value international projects and enter into co-production arrangements for realisation of back-end revenues. Another positive sign is that the industry is gradually moving up the value chain—from work-on-hire arrangements to occupying the gaming and home video space in business.

The gaming industry, though, is still at a nascent stage and, in terms of a global presence, lags far behind the U.S., China, Canada, Australia and Japan. Consumer spending is mainly concentrated in four key disciplines: console gaming (including hand-held games), PC games, online games and wireless games. Console gaming commands two-thirds of the world market share, the biggest manufacturers being in Japan, but the consumers (in terms of popularity) are in the U.S. and Europe. China is regarded as a risky area because of rampant piracy. But with newer editions of PlayStations, DS (dual screen) hand-held players and iQues having in-built security features like flash memory (which are resistant to piracy), many manufacturers are now eyeing the Chinese market with the hope of cracking counterfeiters. Most high-end games these days have memory cards that can be used only with the console with which they are sold.

Then there are the online games accounting for 10 per cent of the market share with South Korea, Taiwan, Japan and China being the biggest players in the sector. In these countries, not only do the subscribers enjoy government support for broadband access but also the manufacturers are encouraged, who give away games free and then charge a subscription fee to play. The latest in this sector is the multiplayer online game (MMOG) that enables hundreds of thousands of players to simultaneously interact in a virtual game world connected by Internet. Its popularity has shot up so dramatically in recent times that the PC gaming market (estimated at 8 per cent) is now on the verge of being rendered extinct.

There is also the wireless gaming market (14 per cent) which draws its strength from the Asia-Pacific region, particularly Japan and South Korea. These two countries have more wireless subscribers than the rest of the world put together. India is fast catching up with them due to the growing usage of mobile handsets and cellular players charging either nothing or a very nominal fee for game downloads. Analysts say that going by the explosive growth in the mobile phone users' base in India, generating gaming content may well become the next big thing to happen in the country after IT outsourcing. Indeed, there are Indian companies which have acquired the franchisee rights of international stars like Pat Cash and Charlie Chaplin for their mobile games and are now turning towards Bollywood for the rights of screen icons like Amitabh Bachchan and Shahrukh Khan. Amazingly, a Chinese company has also been trying to enter this field with plans to release a dozen new gaming products featuring only Hindi film actors.

Mobile Telephony

From running pre-release publicity teasers as text messages to selling ring tones, ring backs, dialer tones, master ring tones and other forms of film music, Bollywood is fast discovering the magic of mobile

telephony. But since the technology is still at a developing stage, its potential has not been fully realised. Many believe this to be the biggest invention since sliced bread and are visualising an era when the simple palm-sized device would determine how film business will be structured, to the extent that three-minute movies, television promos and trailers on the mobile will be the norm. There is also talk of holographic projections, of being able to drive and watch a movie or television programme, of mobile phones cannibalising the box-office, and so on. Such speculation is not altogether far-fetched. Soon enough, we will be outgrowing the stage when a mobile is used for a little more than talking and exchanging text messages or for such routine activities as booking film tickets and taking part in contests.

In the West, the mobile phone is already being employed as a Swiss Army knife—a supermarket of technology with enough storage capacity and software to accommodate everything from family photo albums to corporate presentations to film clips and personal data. Most handset models have a fairly large collection of attractive features like a sizeable screen, a decent camera, good battery life and Bluetooth to cordlessly communicate with a personal computer or headset. As a fashion accessory also, it is finding increasing acceptability among the elderly and pre-teens looking for simplicity and ease of use with a well-edited boutique of technology instead of a supermarket. The recognition that talk is only part of the mobile phone's future—that it is becoming a personal window into an evolving blend of communication systems, computing and media—has the existing players scrambling for more and more tools of higher and higher quality without daring to raise prices. They are all searching for a money-making future beyond talk, which is destined to become a mature business, though highly competitive and progressively less profitable, with time.

So there are wireless carriers rolling out high speed networks that can handle television, movie trailering and music, in addition to all kinds of information, from e-mails to cricket scores to news and

weather updates. Handset makers are introducing the 'next generation' multi-media phone that can not only store up to 3,000 songs,
but will also double up as a high quality camera and a video recorder
capable of shooting and storing an hour of video content. Consequently, media companies worldwide are looking at mobile telephony as a new market for their entertainment, news and search
products. Time-Warner, Google, Yahoo, Microsoft and Viacom are
some of the leading players in the arena. The latest is the music
cellphone designed to extend the music business beyond the iPod.

India, as usual, is adopting a wait-'n'-watch stance, at least till such
time as the dust settles. But technologists and industry analysts are
already talking of three screens—television, personal computer and
mobile phone—each with its strengths and weaknesses. The television screen is best for group entertainment, the PC screen for
browsing the Internet and the mobile phone for combining personal work with play. In this furious battle of the screens, the mobile
phone will doubtless emerge the winner as it is one piece of technology that nobody needs any convincing to buy. It is cheap, versatile,
convenient and easy to use. It is an any-time any-place technology.
Even in a price-sensitive market like India, it has ceased to be a
luxury and has become a must-have, a necessity for most city
dwellers.

The only problem, though, is the confusing and often costly billing
schemes cellphone companies are offering on their networks. As
services go beyond the voice and text mode, pricing becomes more
and more complicated with charges levied by the megabyte. In the
U.S., some carriers have adopted a flat pricing, but with an additional charge beyond basic data services (e-mail, instant messages
and Web access) like the menu of television programming or picture
messaging service. The idea of all-you-can-eat pricing (with one
monthly price for voice and a higher price for data of all kinds) has
not worked in that country.

Another contentious issue is whether to make handsets a personal
device customised to the specific needs of a user or continue in the

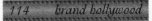

race to make it an all-doing, all-singing, general purpose, everything gadget. An increasingly vocal section of marketing experts has been arguing that people will be better served by a family of devices that will work like a society of personalised machines, the mobile phone being one of them. The counter-view is that if advancements in technology are not suitably exploited, society might as well stick to landlines. In seeking a viable course between these two extremes, some carriers have made the mobile a remote control for the home. The user, while at work or travelling, could set room temperatures, programme the television set, turn on the oven to start the roast and watch the kids doing their homework by viewing the images transmitted from small, inexpensive cameras in each room. Smart chips can also make the phone a credit card with biometric sensors providing fingerprint identification. Furthermore, a person may have three or four phones, all with the same number, which can be used one at a time. He may use a music-centred phone with headphones while jogging or shopping, an office productivity phone for e-mails and taking notes on a business trip, and a stylish phone during evenings while dining out with family and friends.

It will not be long before all these facilities will be available in India and prompt Bollywood producers to rethink their publicity strategies. They already know that the mobile is the only marketing tool that links films with all other media of communication—television, PC, animation and gaming, radio and music. They also realise that teenagers spend more time on their mobiles than adults and have therefore targeted this segment with ring tones, wallpapers, show-time contests, polls for awards' functions and publicity teasers. Kids are also known to be more receptive (if not vulnerable) towards these marketing ploys and tend to take part in them more enthusiastically than their parents. To an extent, such segmentation of the target audience helps in creating a buzz about films in the market.

Much more can be achieved through mobile telephony, except for some issues peculiar to Bollywood which remain to be resolved. For one, there still exists a huge disconnect between content and

know-how, which publicists have not been able to bridge. A campaign on mobile phones becomes most effective when some kind of synergy between the technological and creative aspects is established. For instance, the technology for trailering and running television promos is available, but how many film-makers have applied it on mobile phones? The excuse commonly bandied about is that it is expensive, but the truth is that nobody has the time to get into the nitty-gritty. A publicist usually gets three to four weeks to plan his campaign before a film is released and he would much rather take the tried and tested route of press ads, billboards and television promos than experiment with off-beat devices like mobile phones. Even by the time ring-tones are made available, the movie has invariably run its course in theatres and is, in all likelihood, forgotten.

The second reason for mobiles not really working in film promotions is that its interactive potential has not been fully exploited, especially with adults. That it can engage audiences in a dialogue and, over time, in a relationship, has not been understood by most film-makers. What might begin with a simple SMS could lead to a connection and, finally, to a dinner with the film's lead stars or even a holiday for two in Switzerland—activities which are routinely promoted by film-makers in the West. Aditya Chopra is among the few producers in Mumbai who somewhat understands how such baits on the mobile work. Before him was Ram Gopal Varma, who was the first to use the mobile phone as a publicity weapon when he sent out a series of anonymous SMSs, each supposedly letting out the mystery of his film, *Bhoot* (2003). It led to widespread speculation among the public as to who the killer in the film might be and, eventually, much to the surprise of trade pundits, tickets started selling out weeks in advance. *Bhoot* was a resounding success!

However, for all the power and promises it holds, the mobile can merely help in the publicity build-up of a film and not beyond that. It cannot be the sole publicity tool for the producer. It has to be part of a larger campaign in which the other media like press, radio, television and outdoor advertising have their roles clearly scripted. In that sense, mobile telephony can at best serve as a catalyst in

creating awareness about new releases. Film-making, after all, is about brand building, and brands do not get built by phone calls. Other promotional activities, including positioning and strategising, are just as important in facilitating the process. But on one count mobile phones have scored over all other modes of communication—they have a way of creating a buzz in the market which, inevitably, leads to word-of-mouth publicity. To a marketing man, there cannot be a better form of advertisement than this.

six

Let the Music Play On

Bollywood is unique inasmuch as it is the only film industry in the world that makes such an elaborate song and dance of its music. No mainstream Hindi film is complete without a minimum of six songs, accompanied by the customary running around trees and bushes, the heroine in white drenched to the bone, marriage cele-brations in swirling *ghagra-cholis*, and gym-toned bodies breaking into vigorous displays of colour and calisthenics. Bollywood film-makers do not need an excuse to have such diversions in their story-lines. Earlier, there used to be some application of thought even for a musical interlude; but ever since films have started having 'item numbers', the good old reasoning of songs and dances serving as bridges to link disparate scenes and taking the narrative forward has been cast away. There are, of course, exceptions to this practice, but such 'song-less films' are few and far between. The idea osten-sibly is to provide dramatic relief to the audience, but, in truth, it is to sustain a steady stream of revenue from the music industry—verily the life-support of Bollywood ever since sound entered cinema with *Alam Ara* (1931).

At present though, the music industry is going through an unpre-cedented recession. This has been a worldwide trend for quite some time, as a result of which a series of revenue-enhancing and cost-cutting measures has been put in place by global music majors since the mid-nineties. In India, the industry size shrunk from Rs 13.5 billion to less that Rs 10 billion in barely four years between

2001 and 2005. Earlier, during the mid-nineties, sale of music rights accounted for as much as 15 per cent of an individual film's earnings and, in certain cases, the revenue was enough to take care of a full-fledged production budget. At that time, there were a lot of instances when producers, even before signing the director, cast and crew, recorded the songs of their film and financed their production with the sale of CDs and cassettes. The onslaught of piracy, high acquisition costs of music rights and low priority accorded to film music by the listening public have since dealt a death blow to the Indian music industry.

Moreover, the pattern of music consumption has radically shifted in recent times. Music buying has reduced and, despite the rising popularity of new Hindi films, the number of units being sold is falling sharply. At an all-India level, new Hindi film music accounts for 40 per cent of the industry pie while old film music claims 21 per cent and regional (non-Hindi) 5 per cent. As for the remaining 34 per cent, devotional music commands the highest share (10 per cent), followed by non-film numbers, international pop and others (8 per cent each). Now relate this to the genre-wise distribution in the English-speaking world. There, film music does not find a place anywhere. Rock music claims the largest market share (27 per cent), followed by pop, rap/hip hop, R&B urban and country, each claiming 12 per cent on an average. The balance is shared among religious music, jazz and classical, in that order.

Obviously, no direct comparison can be made between these two world markets. Tastes are different, and so are the cultures. But the issues plaguing them are common. In both, piracy has ensured that the average retail price of music cassettes over the years remains stagnant while that of CDs keeps falling. As the consequent slump has not been compensated by rising volumes, revenue from the industry is on a continual tailspin. India has to additionally contend with a rapid rise of remixes, cover versions and music videos based on original soundtracks. Significantly, these have found great popularity with the masses and receive more airplay than the originals on television and radio, but they do not impact sales to any appreciable

extent. Leakage of royalty income is further compounded by digital downloads and mobile ring-tones, on which there has been no check so far. While experts have suggested the leveraging of appropriate technology in order to tap the swing in audience preferences, the unfortunate fact is that the Indian music industry does not have any control on its own distribution and manufacturing costs. It continues to be bogged down by huge investments in infrastructure with absolutely no solution in sight for either freeing the trapped capital or enhancing its bottom-line in the immediate future. Until such time as the various stakeholders including film producers and the many user-segments get together and adopt a collaborative approach towards a financial rejuvenation, there can be little hope for the industry to hit the path of recovery. Eventually, the biggest beneficiaries of a healthy and robust music industry are none other than Bollywood producers themselves. Emerging from this are three key areas of collaboration which demand immediate attention:

- Drawing up a participative business model, whereby film producers and music companies share the risks and rewards on an equitable basis.

- Higher investments by various industry segments in using digital technology and digital formats for distribution in order to limit physical piracy.

- Expanding the organised market by opening large format retail outlets (stocking legitimate music), targeting select consumer segments and reducing distribution and ancillary costs.

Now let us examine what the ground realities are and whether, in recent times, the music and film industries have been mutually supportive:

Revenue Sharing

Instead of offering film producers guarantees of sale as in the past, music companies are now proposing to share revenue from royalty. This way, the latter are playing safe and covering up for possible losses from poor sale and piracy. Film-makers, who were accustomed

to being paid huge sums on grossly over-rated music, have consequently become more cautious and are insisting on added reassur-
ances that royalties would flow in, even in trickles, for all time.
Mahesh Bhatt entered into one such royalty sharing arrangement
in 2004 for his film, *Murder*, starring Emraan Hashmi and Mallika
Sherawat. Luckily for him and the music company, one solo number
by a new playback singer, Kunal Ganjawala, became the chartbuster
of the season and turned the fortunes of the film around.

Switching Tracks

So long as all was hunky dory—till the mid-nineties—film producers
had a cosy thing going with music companies of their choice. It
meant that they automatically entrusted the music rights of whichever film they made to one or the other company, and no questions
were asked. Enduring relationships of trust and mutual dependence
were built in this manner. For instance, the music of all Yash Chopra
films was handled for several decades by the HMV-Saregama group.
In 2004, with *Veer–Zaara*, Chopra suddenly decided to snap connections with HMV and released the music of the film under his
own label, Yash Raj Music. Soon, Subhash Ghai followed suit and
launched his own music company with *Kisna* (2005). Then other
producers like Suneel Darshan and the Sahara group took off on
their own. Chopra somehow got lucky and made a killing on the
music of *Veer–Zaara* (2004), but the others were not so fortunate
and are still aimlessly floundering in the dark. This is because they
do not realise that their core competence lies in film-making and
not in hawking music cassettes and CDs. They are neither familiar
with ground realities nor equipped with the expertise necessary to
handle the complexities of a market monopolised for generations
by a few well-entrenched families. This me-unto-myself attitude is
costing both Bollywood and the music industry dearly.

Non-film Music

One reason for the music industry not resisting the intrusion of
film producers into its turf is that remixes, albums of non-playback
artistes, devotionals and other music categories have virtually

flooded the film music market. This had never happened before. Film-makers believe that things have been allowed to come to such a pass simply because music companies were not pushy enough in promoting film music and, in every other aspect, turned out to be completely laidback about the way they conducted their businesses. To a major extent, this is true. Owners of several music companies had harboured ambitions of turning into full-fledged film producers and, in pursuing this objective, neglected their core business. By the time they realised their folly, the rug had been pulled from under their feet and it was too late to make amends.

Copyright Disputes

Whether it is a full-time music company or a two-timing film-maker dealing with music sales, certain disputes have persisted over time. The most common relates to revenue sharing with FM broadcasters for the music played on radio channels. (The latter are accusing music companies of violating contracts by holding back their music.) Hotels and restaurants constitute the second contentious area, particularly on the issue of playing copyrighted music during occasions, like New Years' Eve and product launches, and not paying the necessary license fees. Live event management companies make for the third litigious group as they refuse to part with revenues earned from playing music at stage shows and concerts. The biggest problem with these disputes is that there are no effective watchdog organisations monitoring the copyright violations and it is always one man's word against another that invariably leads to acrimonious and inconclusive arguments. The Indian Performing Rights Society (IPRS) is there, but it is so severely constrained by resources and manpower that it has failed to make much of a difference in resolving any dispute.

Digital Music

In the overlapping of activities between music companies and film producers, what has gone clearly unnoticed is the advent of digitisation of recorded music. Neither has drawn any real advantage from this mini revolution as yet. Digital music still accounts for 1 to 2 per cent share of the total industry revenues, whereas in the West, newer

formats are hitting the market with every passing week. One such popular format is the dual disc, which has an audio CD on one side and a DVD on the other. The album is enhanced with 5.1 Surround Sound or DVD-Audio and the DVD side contains additional material, such as, photos, interviews, lyrics, biographical material and videos showing the making of the album. Another popular innovation is the iTunes Music Store, which was launched by Apple in April 2003 and, within 12 months, recorded its 200 millionth download. The popularity of the iPod portable device has further stimulated interest in the service. Now it is legally possible to access songs online on the same day as they are introduced in the market and, at times, even prior to their physical release, thanks to the optimal exploitation of digital services. These are opportunities going abegging for the Indian film industry.

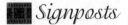 Signposts

In a music loving country like India, licensed digital distribution is the only foreseeable solution for getting the music industry up by the bootstraps and, in effect, realising its potential. Distribution of mobile ring-tones and caller music is supposed to offer another lucrative possibility, both for film producers and music companies. Already we are witnessing school and college kids who, in addition to making calls, playing games, clicking pictures and sending text messages, are using the mobile phone to play music as they do with the Walkman. The odd part is that there are no reliable means of monitoring the quantum of musical downloads, let alone place a correct price for the facility. For that matter, the entire music industry in India operates under a cloak of secrecy as nobody reveals details of unit sales and average realisation prices. Consequently, no accurate figure can ever be pegged on the size of the industry. On a very rough estimate though, Indian music companies were said to have generated approximately 150 million legitimate unit sale of cassettes and CDs in 2004 with an average realisation of

Rs 40 to Rs 45 per unit. On this basis, the size of the industry was taken to be Rs 6.7 billion (not including royalty earnings) in that year. Also, for purely statistical computation, a figure of 3 per cent is quoted as the average annual growth rate estimated for the industry between 2001 and 2010.

While there could be many reasons for music company owners to remain secretive about their scale of operations, a few signposts indicating the direction they are heading towards have shown up. Recognising these indicators would be of immense help to Bollywood producers while formulating their business strategies:

Talent Sourcing

In the earlier days, radio used to be a fertile ground for spotting and nurturing musical talent. Most top-selling albums, till recently, were of instrumentalists and vocalists who had initially cut their musical teeth as radio artistes. Now that public attention has shifted to television, and with Bollywood being the dream destination for every upcoming artiste in India, music companies have abandoned the radio for sourcing talent. Certain contests and reality shows like Zee TV's *Sa Re Ga Ma Pa* and Sony's *Indian Idol* are indicative of what the future holds for the music and film industries. All such programmes are heavily loaded with film content, as contestants are expected to be sound-alikes of yesteryear playback artistes like Lata Mangeshkar, Kishore Kumar, Mohammad Rafi, Asha Bhonsle and others. Regardless of the number of contests being held on the same format, there is never a lack of viewership for such musical programmes, and with it ad revenues have zoomed and career prospects have opened up for the winners. Above all, stars are born for music companies in this manner.

Music Videos

Traditionally, the Indian music industry has ridden piggy-back on film music. New or old, Hindi or non-Hindi, playback singers have always been the staple human resource on which music companies have survived. Even today, for every cassette or CD of a non-film

album sold, there are at least two customers waiting to pick up the album of a playback artiste. But then, nobody can be sure about how long this trend will last. The advent of satellite television has created hitherto non-existent platforms for non-film music channels and, in turn, music videos. With their popularity, the market share of their revenues vis-à-vis total industry revenues is also steadily rising. Some music videos like *Sweet Honey Mix* (2004), *Ek Haseena Thi* (2004) and *Miss Spicy Mix* (2004) have made superstars out of lead dancers like Shefali Zariwala and Negar Khan. People are choosing to buy cassettes and CDs of their remixed versions over the originals (mainly for playing at parties, discotheques and restaurants) simply by association of the visuals with the music. There are also accomplished singers like Baba Sehgal and Shubha Mudgal who have similarly taken the music video route for promoting their non-film albums. Now, film producers are resorting to the same gimmick by shooting 'item numbers' for a television audience, regardless of whether they are required for the film or not. Such is the power of television in promoting music.

Synergy with Radio

Television may be the preferred medium for music promotion, but radio has not altogether lost its importance. With the advent of private FM channels, a new area for the growth of music content is opening up. These broadcasters are forever starved of the latest musical hits, mainly from films, in order to beat competition and retain the loyalty of listeners. It is much like the earlier days when film music was the main driver for All India Radio's commercial service, Vividh Bharati. And this is what the advertisers also insist on. Unlike television, where non-film songs (read music videos) might have an edge, in radio, film music rules supreme and commands the highest premium in air time bookings with advertisers. At another level, both music companies and film producers are finding this a perfect low-cost marketing platform (as compared to other media), ideally suited for music launches. With the government out to auction more and more frequencies as part of its expansion plans, FM radio could well serve as the necessary growth catalyst for the Indian music industry in the future.

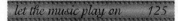

Shelf Life

Gone are the days when the shelf life of film music extended to several months, if not years. There used to be depth and substance in the lyrics, orchestration, melody and recording of songs, which together contributed to an almost everlasting appeal for yesteryears' classics. Today, one in a thousand film songs would qualify to be an all-time hit. The rest are recorded in a tearing hurry with no imagination and very bad singers, lyricists and music composers. So if the shelf life of film music has shrunk to a few days or weeks, the cause is not the change in listeners' tastes, but the quality of the product. The tragedy of the situation is that for acquiring the rights of such sub-standard products, music companies are parting with astronomical sums in the hope that possibly one out of ten numbers may click. In this gamble, they are going bust, but the composers and singers are laughing all the way to the bank. Taking advantage of this situation are the mindless remix racketeers, who are commanding a far larger share of the overall music industry than the composers of original soundtracks. Little wonder then that many film producers like Subhash Ghai and Ram Gopal Varma are themselves preparing remixed versions of their own songs within weeks of the release of the original, lest someone else 'steals' it. At times, there are two or three remixed versions of the same song in circulation, almost simultaneously.

Album Unbundling

Many Indian music companies are now turning to what is commonly understood in the trade as 'unbundling of albums'. Very simply, this means that consumers do not have to pay for an entire collection of songs in an album, but can pick and choose what they want and thereby reduce their music acquisition costs. This move has been prompted by the emergence of relatively newer delivery platforms, such as, the Internet, whereby people can purchase individual songs of their liking and create their own albums. Earlier, music lovers had to put up with junk in a collection for the sake of one or two good numbers of their choice. They had no alternative and music companies found this to be the most convenient way of pushing songs

for which there were otherwise no takers. Now they are realising how self-defeating the practice was. Besides, album unbundling results in lower delivery costs and, ultimately, higher margins.

Product Expansion

Over the years, music companies have discovered that music sales alone cannot sustain profitability. As such, they are increasingly getting into allied segments like VCDs and DVDs by acquiring combined rights from producers. Also, at the retailing level, they are clubbing offers with cinema tickets and other promotional merchandise. Some are entering into tie-ups with coffee chains and book publishing houses. This leveraging of each other's strengths has not only brought about a level of corporatisation in the distribution segment of the music industry, but it is also contributing to the efforts of checking piracy and increasing the availability of legitimate music content. More than anything else, these collaborative efforts with the film industry, both at the production and distribution level, have reduced acquisition costs for the music companies and, in turn, raised their profitability.

Overseas Potential

The curiosity generated by the so-called 'crossover films' among Indian expatriates towards Bollywood cinema has opened the doors for the Indian music industry to a huge overseas market hitherto unexplored. It is a market where licensed digital distribution and mobile music are ruling the roost; where music is routinely integrated into video games and game producers are licensing relatively unknown artistes who are less expensive than the big name acts; where demand for music videos has flattened out; and where new ways for promoting artistes have played a key role in generating excitement in local industries and stimulated sales. Exposure to all these experiences will, no doubt, hold the Indian music industry in good stead and the lessons learnt would, in turn, be transferred to Bollywood. The fact is that no matter how resolutely the two industries try to chart their own independent courses, they will always have to remain beholden and supportive of one another. One just cannot do without the other.

◼ Partnering Progress

At the grass-roots level, music serves as the first point of contact for a film-maker with the masses. That is why music launches are elaborate star-studded events every Bollywood producer must necessarily organise before getting into the brand building of his film. Several bad and indifferent films in Bollywood history have performed beyond expectations, purely on the strength of superlative music tracks. The reverse is also true—countless good films have floundered at the box-office in the absence of adequate musical support. This happens because music companies, who are better equipped than film-makers in feeling the pulse of the market, do not have any say whatsoever in the way music is conceived and produced. Film-makers are people driven by emotions, whereas music companies are run by hard-nosed businessmen, motivated by cold, calculative minds. The two disciplines are mutually exclusive, unless a producer, gifted with an ear for music (like Raj Kapoor, Yash Chopra or Subhash Ghai) comes along and strikes a common chord between the heart and the head. That is when everlasting hits are created, both for the film producer and the music industry.

Since these are one-off events that cannot be counted on, a collaborative approach based on revenue sharing and understanding (as indicated earlier) would be the only sensible course open to both industries. Till such time as music companies are involved in the content-creation at the film-making stage and producers become equally accountable for marketing the music, any form of co-operation will be meaningless. Revenue sharing has to be necessarily combined with risk taking for any collaborative effort to succeed. Of course, the easier way out is for producers to take up music distribution and launch their own music companies, the way some have already done. But that is not a wise alternative to work on, as markets have already proved.

There is another major advantage that will come out of the envisaged teamwork of music company owners and film-makers.

A unified effort is bound to bring about a price correction on the purchase of music rights. Significantly, while the film industry has been going through a phase of rationalisation over the past several years, the music industry is inexplicably making some over-valued acquisitions. The risk here is that the moment a film-maker sees his revenue stream drying up from any such price correction, he will promptly turn his back on the music company. Trade analysts, therefore, believe that in the long run, Bollywood will witness some major acquisitions instead of alliances, with some top film production houses taking over music companies to avail of their distribution network and operational expertise.

It is also believed within the music industry that the proliferation of private FM radio stations across the country will eventually lead to a decline in the sales of cassettes and CDs. This apprehension is, however, completely unfounded. Across the globe, radio, by repeatedly playing musical hits, has only helped in promoting albums and labels. In India, the reverse is considered true because of two reasons: One, FM came in at a time when the music industry was already slipping into a depression. And two, the genre preference of the Indian listener is uniquely skewed towards new film music. It is also true that in cities where FM has not yet reached, it is not as though music sales have gone up even marginally. The slump is consistent across India, regardless of whether listeners have access to FM radio or not.

This brings us to the second area of strategic alliance for the music industry. Whether anybody likes it or not, radio is developing into a major industry with private broadcasters all set to eclipse the state-run All India Radio. So, instead of being at loggerheads, music and radio have to, by necessity, find a common ground for co-existence and better still, draw up a shared growth plan for the future. To give an example, the possibilities for synergy through co-branding of music products and properties can be explored with the private FM radio broadcasters. For starters, Radio A could promote a collection of X Music's songs or artistes, resulting in an increase in the demand for such songs. In return, X Music could release a *Radio A Top 10* album consisting of the most popular songs and programmes

promoted on air. Likewise, from city to city, there could be a *Radio B Top 10*, *Radio C Top 10* and so on. The possibilities are endless. Even non-film songs of good quality, which may otherwise not find a suitable airtime for broadcast, can be promoted in this manner. Alternatively, through intelligent revenue sharing arrangements, the radio channel may be offered incentives to provide airtime to experimental and off-beat music which need promotion.

The third possibility of collaborative marketing would be in the area of online sales. With PC penetration going up by the day, the Internet will play an increasingly proactive role in influencing music purchases in the future. After all, it must be understood, music is not a 'must have' item in the shopping list of most Indians. It is neither a necessity nor is there anything like brand loyalty for a particular music label in this country. What counts is convenience. If a piece of interesting music, heard on the radio or from a neighbour's house can be acquired at the click of the mouse, chances are the listener will go for it. This way, through online sales, music companies will incur lower distribution costs and actually save the 15–20 per cent margins set aside for retailers. Part of the savings can be utilised for innovative Net-marketing that offers consumers detailed information and reviews, as also the facility of customised and unbundled offerings. The future demands a new consumer-inspired business model that incorporates everything that modern technology has to offer, coupled with enhanced retail delivery systems at lower prices. Since this requires significant investments in terms of time and money, ideally all major music labels will have to agree to come together and put their repertoire on common downloadable platforms. Better still, they could work together with digital access providers to homes, through cable, fibre or satellite on a joint revenue sharing basis.

Emerging home entertainment technologies, the growth of high-end mobile handsets and the increasingly dominant role of music in games, advertising, television and corporate events only means that music companies have to reinvent themselves and re-engage innovatively with consumers from time to time. Even at the level of

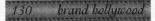

traditional music selling at retail outlets, innovation holds the key. The advent of hypermarkets, multiplexes and other entertainment destinations has changed the way business is done. Globally, these large format retail stores account for 40 per cent of music sales, whereas in India, despite increasing footfalls, it is less than 2 per cent. Only now are we learning to bundle music with offerings of books and coffee and, in some cases, by extending the point of sales to car service and petrol stations as well as electronics shops. This is essentially to take advantage of the fact that for most Indians, the purchase of entertainment products is usually guided by the twin factors of impulse and convenience.

Indian music companies can also learn from the experiences of their Western counterparts who have adopted the marketing models developed by FMCG (fast moving consumer goods) companies to launch and sell lifestyle products. In a way, music is also a lifestyle product. So it is conceivable that once brand loyalty is established, music companies can similarly charge a premium for the product from target audiences. This applies to both film and non-film albums. In the case of the latter though, a good deal of A&R (artiste and repertoire) management will become necessary. Notable experiments in A&R were visible in the case of music groups, Viva and Band of Boys, when music and television companies joined hands to create a talent pool of artistes capable of creating differentiated music content in the market. The artistes were groomed, promoted and retained by the label, and with the added support of television, they not only became singing stars in double quick time, but more importantly, they began to serve as brand ambassadors for the music labels. Apart from generating music sales, the creation of brands can be leveraged for several other sources of revenue like brand merchandise and memorabilia, among other things. At the same time, the cost of such talent acquisition is relatively low, as compared to the fee and royalties required to be paid to established singing stars.

As for film albums, the growing popularity of remixes is working as a double-edged sword for the music industry. On the one hand, the tunes of yesteryears' hits are being filched, doctored and released without as much as an acknowledgement to the original composer, singer and music label. On the other hand, parent companies have now found a new window of opportunity and, thus, getting into the remix act in a big way. So encouraging have the results been that they are getting bolder by the day and even remixing old devotional and classical numbers with unknown (though not always untalented) artistes under their own label. No doubt, these are huge money-spinners today. But somehow, somewhere, everybody knows that grave injustice is being done to the original artistes and composers by these remixed numbers. They get no share of the profits and, worse, have to bear the anguish of their music being butchered ... in silence. There is no forum for redressal for such blatant abuse of intellectual property.

 ## Music Theft

The Phonographic Performance Ltd (PPL) and the IPRS are two industry bodies responsible for monitoring copyright violations and royalty collection of all music publicly played over radio and tele-vision, in restaurants, clubs, discotheques, and so on. Remixes do not come under their purview as these are promoted as inspired, if not original, compositions. Ethically and otherwise, they ought to be treated as infringements of copyright. But when the Indian Copyright Act was drawn up in 1956, nobody had anticipated that remixes would become so big and snowball into such a contentious issue. Today, some kind of a unholy pact persists between the film industry and music companies, whereby an embargo automatically falls into place on the release of a music for a period of two years only. After this period, anybody is free to remix any film song in any manner without seeking permission of the original rights holder. The funny part is that the rights holders themselves are remixing their songs without waiting for the two years to elapse. Subhash Ghai, for instance, released the remixed version of a song from *Aetraaz* (produced under his banner) almost simultaneously with the original in 2004!

On the issue of royalty collections though, the role and efficiency of IPRS has been commendable. Awareness of piracy and its risks have consequently gone up over the years as many defaulters have been brought to book. Music companies, which had virtually given up on the pirates, are now suddenly waking up to substantial revenues pouring in as royalties from a vast cache of users. Ironically enough, most of these music companies were themselves pirates at one time and had made their millions before going legit in recent years. Their knowledge about the intricacies of piracy and market dynamics has enabled both PPL and IPRS to track down offenders and claiming the industry's dues to a large extent. Otherwise, with their limited manpower and infrastructure, it would have been extremely difficult for PPL and IPRS to constantly monitor copyright violations and recover royalties on a nation-wide scale.

There is also a judicial angle to this. The law prescribes punishments for a term of not less than six months and a fine of over Rs 50,000 for all copyright violations. In reality, offenders manage to get away with, at the most, a single day imprisonment and fines between Rs 500 and Rs 1,000. In some cases, even these basic penalties are not enforced. And when fines are imposed, the money goes to the government's coffers and not to the aggrieved music companies. Coupled with the leniency of the courts is the absence of optical disc laws, whereby the original rights holders stand to lose every time a copy of a popular song is made by another recording company. Smaller recording companies and new entrants, without significant archival content have successfully exploited this aspect and prospered at the expense of the original rights holders. They have also brought about huge losses to the exchequer by non-payment of income tax, sales tax, excise duties and entertainment tax.

Furthermore, the PPL and IPRS have been campaigning for a tighter regulatory regime and more stringent enforcement of law to block revenue leakages caused by piracy. On the related concern of increasing collections and bringing more users in the royalty net, one solution could be to introduce a point of sales tax—a levy charged from all patrons of pubs, discotheques, entertainment shows, etc., along with the ticket price and added to the share of revenue of

the establishments. At the end of the year, this collection can be distributed among various music companies, depending upon their audited accounts or on the basis of a commonly agreed ratio. This way, not only would a degree of transparency set into the industry, but more importantly, music companies would get their royalties in a spirit of justice and fair play. A part of the money collected through this means could perhaps be retained in a common corpus that may, among other things, help in intensifying piracy control measures and public awareness campaigns.

Of late, a national task force has also been set up under the aegis of the Federation of Indian Chambers of Commerce and Industry (FICCI) to combat counterfeiting and piracy of music. Some of the measures recently initiated by it are as follows:

- Anti-piracy campaigns: These include the release of press-ads, running public awareness messages on radio and television and putting up outdoor hoardings featuring celebrities urging the public to desist from purchasing pirated music.

- Creating awareness within the music industry and outside on the stipulations of the Copyright Act and drawing up plans and programmes for its implementation more vigorously, particularly in non-metros where piracy is rampant.

- Supporting international copyright conventions like IFPI (International Federation of the Phonographic Industry), which represents recording industries worldwide with over 1,450 members in 75 countries and affiliated industry associations in 48 countries and World Intellectual Property Organisation (WIPO).

- Promoting digital technologies, like the use of holograms on cassettes and CDs, to safeguard the interests of consumers (who can distinguish between the original and a counterfeit at the point of purchase) and music companies.

- Monitoring the manufacture of CDs, which, for reasons of high sound quality, low pricing and better value for money have become increasingly popular across the country. Today, more pirated music is available on CDs than cassettes.

In all this, the attitude of the government is rather strange. Either it does not recognise music piracy to be such a serious offence or it could just not be bothered. The latter possibility is more likely, because it has virtually no stakes (apart from the usual taxes it recovers) in the music industry. The ministry of information and broadcasting in New Delhi does not even have the faintest idea about the magnitude of the problem. Let alone creating a department to deal with the menace, it has not even set up an anti-piracy cell for the music industry. For cinema—even as it is supposed to be in the private sector—the government holds huge interests in the form of supporting several white elephants like Films Division, National Film Development Corporation, Children's Film Society of India, National Film Archive of India and, of course, the Central Board of Film Certification or Censor Board. Even the press has to bear with government intervention, whether through the Press Information Bureau or the Registrar of Newspapers. But for the music industry, there is no state intervention, support or protection. Good or bad, it is left to its own devices and has to fend for itself through thick and thin.

The only consolation the music industry can draw is that music piracy in India has not yet reached the levels prevalent in certain other parts of the world. The People's Republic of China is said to be a pirate's paradise with counterfeits accounting for more than 90 per cent of music stores sales. Indonesia comes next with an estimated 65 per cent incidence rate, followed by Malaysia and Pakistan at the 50 per cent mark. India falls in the category of Hong Kong, the Philippines, Taiwan and Thailand, which have piracy levels in excess of 25 per cent, while Australia, Japan and New Zealand are the only countries where the incidence is less than 10 per cent.

In the West, where vigilance is high, piracy has been under control but never really wiped out. This is primarily because of the common phenomenon of technology overtaking legislation and newer devices being invented now and then to bypass the laws. On the other hand, the prices of genuine music CDs and cassettes have been deliberately kept so low as to render piracy a non-profitable

and high-risk venture. This could be effective in the U.S., U.K. and parts of Europe where English music is appreciated due to the fact that sales volumes in the category of pop music are so huge that lower margins are easily taken care of by the numbers. That apart, regular raids leading to seizure and court proceedings have conclusively put the fear of prosecution in the pirates. In February 2004, Australia seized replicating material from KaZaA and several universities for violations of copyright laws. Raids were also conducted against four Internet service providers, including the reputed Telstra Corp.

Elsewhere, in China, Warner Music has slashed prices on select music albums by as much as two-thirds to minimise the possibilities of pirated copies showing up. Likewise, the Malaysian government has imposed a price ceiling on all cassettes and CDs produced in the country, leading to an unprecedented boom in its music industry. Now, the governments of other Asian countries like South Korea, Indonesia and Thailand are following suit. All these governments have finally come to terms with the fact that plain economic factors exert a far greater influence on violations of the law than any amount of legislation and litigation put together. After all, crime thrives only when its commission is profitable.

seven

Crime and Punishment

Mechanically reproducing recordings of someone else's work and passing it as one's own is not the only crime Bollywood music pirates are notorious for. Copying and incorporating tunes—even lyrics— without acknowledgement is as widely prevalent and is as much of an offence. So is the common practice of downloading music from the Net without payment or permission. Unauthorised use of film music as ring-tones in mobile phones also amounts to infringement of the laws relating to intellectual property rights. Even playing, singing, whistling or humming a few notes of a copyrighted musical work in a film, tele-serial or an advertising commercial would re-quire the permission of the composer or the original rights holder. Let alone films and commercials, reproducing musical works for video games and mechanical toys would also attract the provisions of the Indian Copyright Act. Everybody commits such crimes with impunity.

But does anybody really care? Sadly, the trouble with most of us is that we choose either to be unaware about legalities or decide to take our chances come what may. We prefer to go with the flow, little realising that one day, the tide could turn against us. When a film-maker commissions a musical work, he expects the composer to come up with an original piece of recording for which he pays (apart from the commissioning fee) a certain amount of money to purchase the copyright for perpetuity. He is not expected to pay the composer any further royalties other than perhaps mechanicals from the sale

of the soundtrack album. These details are generally listed in the terms of contract entered between the producer and music composer. Effectively, the producer acquires the right to record the composition in synchronisation with the soundtrack of the film and to make copies of the recordings in such formats as are necessary for the theatrical exhibition of the film or for transmission on television, video, VCD/DVD players and so on. He does not have the right to alter the composition to suit his fancy, use it for another film, adapt or adopt the lyrics of the composition separately for himself or even part with the rights to another film-maker or composer. For all this, he will require the consent of the composer and there is a certain procedure, by law, for going about it. But how many producers and composers actually want to know or care about these finer details? Just because 'others' are committing a crime and getting away with it, they want to believe it is legitimate. They do not even realise that in doing so, they remain constantly exposed to penalisation by law and being unfairly exploited by unscrupulous elements any time.

In Bollywood, the work culture is such that everybody makes pretence of being busy and getting on with the job at hand. The rest is left to the Almighty or destiny. A composer will steal a music track from his colleague and will keep hoping against hope that he does not get caught the next morning. The film-maker who buys the composition may be aware that he is paying for a plagiarised work, but he will keep his mouth shut, hoping that the original composer turns stone deaf or, better still, dies in his sleep. Chances are that the latter himself has stolen the music from a more distant source and nobody knows about it as yet. In any case, the film-maker should be the last person to point an accusing finger at anybody because, in all probability, he himself could be guilty of producing a frame-by-frame copy of a foreign pot-boiler. In this brotherhood of copycats, nothing is legit and each one lives by his wits and a silent prayer that he survives the day as a free man. The Indian Copyright Act may well be damned anyway.

There is another reason for nobody taking cognisance of the Copyright Act. When the law was enacted, the basic purpose was

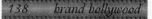

to provide a legislative framework to stimulate and support creativity, as well as to ensure that the creators of intellectual property were suitably rewarded. For the social, cultural and economic growth of a modern civilised society, basic safeguards against theft of creative works was considered necessary. Today also, the same concerns hold good but it is in their implementation that questions of validity are being raised. How, for instance, do you enforce the Copyright Act against digital theft? At a time when digitisation has become the *mantra* of the entertainment industry, who is really bothered about what the law permits or not? So long as you get better value for money, nothing else seems to matter.

Everybody knows that no law holds any relevance in an online environment. Internet is a vibrant medium and anybody wanting to enforce a watertight law to regulate it will be frustrated. If, for instance, Google were to be declared a paid service tomorrow, would it really work? Some geek somewhere would find a way to crack the security code and surfers will continue to access it free of charge. Even the World Intellectual Property Organisation (WIPO), with all the support of its 183 member states, has realised the futility of enforcing a global regulatory framework in the face of advancements of technology. It could do nothing during the Athens Olympics in 2004 when television signals were intercepted by non-subscribers and beamed across the world. These days, Indian television companies are helplessly watching the interception of signals of Hindi sitcoms and cricket matches by unauthorised agents abroad and beamed clandestinely for the benefit of Indian expatriates. Whatever the legal restrictions, technology always finds a way to circumvent them.

Film piracy, however, is a different ball game altogether. At one level, it assumes the simple expedience of stealing the story and structure of a film, without acknowledgement. Scores of Hindi filmmakers have made a fortune through these means, especially by plagiarising past classics and proven box-office hits from other languages. And there is nothing anybody is able do about it because it can always be argued that no frame, let alone the entire film, can

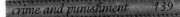

be an exact copy of another. The ones who do get hauled up in court are those who flick stories from a published or registered work and the author gets wind of it. But even there, it is virtually impossible to pin anybody down as the legal processes are so tenuous and loaded in favour of the guilty that invariably the aggrieved party succumbs to an out-of-court settlement. No Indian court has ever imposed an injunction on the release of a Hindi film whose origins have been contested.

The other level at which film piracy occurs is when a print finds its way into the hands of someone who makes multiple copies, invariably on video or CDs. It can happen anywhere—in a processing lab, projection room, studio, cow shed, and even while the film cans are in transit from one theatre to another. How this happens is anybody's guess. In the past, a pirated print could easily be detected from the poor picture and sound quality. But these days, with the availability of incredibly advanced, high-speed replicating machines, it has become almost impossible to differentiate between the original and a copy. The best way of checking out the level of sophistication that film piracy has reached is to pick up any print of the latest Bollywood pot-boiler in circulation from neighbouring Pakistan. There, almost all Indian films are officially banned; so whatever is available has most likely reached through underground channels. But not even a trained eye can distinguish between a smuggled print and a copy. The oddest part is that all these pirated prints reach Lahore and Karachi even before the film is formally released in India. Small wonder then that Indian pirates are sourcing their merchandise from Pakistan these days. They are getting better quality CDs, at cheaper rates and faster than anybody else can legitimately deliver in India.

In the circumstances, the only obvious way to beat the pirates at their game is by rendering their business unprofitable. As mentioned in the earlier chapter, if the original can be priced cheaper than the contraband, the latter will have no takers. At one time (before DVDs and VCDs became popular), producers and distributors believed that instead of phasing out the release of a film over an extended

period of time across different distribution territories, it would be better to carpet bomb the entire country with multiple prints simultaneously. That way nobody could feel deprived, and before the pirates got into their act, everybody interested would have watched the film on the big screen in the theatres. Today, the same strategy is being adopted for DVDs and VCDs. But where the producers are losing out is on the pricing and, at times, on the indifferent quality of the CDs. With so many intermediaries down the distribution chain, the producer cannot slash the retail price beyond a certain point. At that price, the consumer usually gets pirated prints of two films of equally good, if not better, picture quality. Worse, the producer is forever confused over the timing of the DVD/VCD release. Releasing it too early could rob him of his theatre earnings and releasing it too late would give the pirates that much more time to get the better of him. Even a day's difference can tip the scales one way or the other. Indians are not known to be a discriminating lot when it comes to quality. What primarily matters for any consumer is the pricing of a product and, second, the privilege of acquiring it before everybody else. And that is where the pirates hold a decisive edge over film-makers.

Government Intervention

The law governing film piracy is pretty clear and on paper appears fairly stringent. But in reality, the Indian Copyright Act is much like the proverbial tiger without teeth. Pirates go about their business knowing well that except for the local beat constable, there is no government machinery in existence to implement the law. And in that rare case when a raid is conducted, it is only a matter of hours before a bail can be secured and they are back in business the next morning. The punishment for being caught red-handed for making copies of films is so mild that far from serving as a deterrent, the provisions of the Act have become a running joke in the industry. Only recently have some state governments imposed the Goonda Act

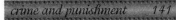

on film pirates, and with the IPRS (Indian Performing Rights Society) intensifying its raids, film producers are beginning to breathe easy. But then, for anybody to imagine that film piracy can ever be wiped off completely from the Indian subcontinent is nothing short of a pipe dream.

Film censorship is another critical area where laws are stringent and the intention of the government is pretty clear. Very simply, it wants to exercise a modicum of control on the film industry, even as it militates against the spirit of democracy and the right to freedom of expression enshrined in the Constitution. As in the case of film piracy, it again does not know how to go about enforcing its authority. The Cinematograph Act of 1952 provides for certain 'censorship guidelines' (open to revision from time to time) that are supposed to restrain film-makers from carrying scenes of a sexually salacious, violent or politically provocative nature for public exhibition. Actually, there are 19 such prohibitive clauses in the Act, but members of the Central Board of Film Certification (CBFC) or the Censor Board are fixated on just these three, or, more specifically, on one, that is, sex. The funny part about the many restrictions is that should a film-maker choose to defy the Board and splice a film (technically, 'interpolate') with deleted or uncensored portions, the chances of him getting caught are one in a million. The government has no means to ensure that a film bearing a censor certificate is screened in accordance with what the Board, in its infinite wisdom, has passed. In fact, apart from the CBFC and the concerned film-maker, nobody ever gets to know in what shape a film has been cleared for public exhibition.

Thus, it should come as no surprise if someone reports a version of a film he/she has seen that is different from what you would have watched in your neighbourhood multiplex. For that matter, if you venture into a mofussil town or, say, somewhere in the interiors of Bihar or Uttar Pradesh, you could well be treated to yet another version of the same film. And do not blink if, in the course of a screening, some alien characters abruptly enter the frame and indulge in heavy petting, nudity and fornication that bear no

relevance whatsoever to the narrative. In film industry parlance, these interpolated sections are the 'bits' that fellow members of the audience have been anxiously waiting for. Screening these un-censored portions is completely illegal and punishable by the Cine-matograph Act, with extended jail terms and heavy fines. But such offences take place everywhere and at all times in collusion with the local police.

There is another way for film-makers to beat the law. Two versions of the same film are shot, using the same cast and crew, locations and even storyline. For one version, some sexually explicit scenes are shot without digressing too far from the plot, while for the other, these scenes are deleted or substituted with song and dance se-quences, flashbacks or some such filler. It is this sanitised version that the film-maker submits to the Censor Board and obtains a clearance certificate. The certificate is then attached to the first version and the film is released for public exhibition. In the absence of a single spliced shot involving extraneous characters, not even the projectionist (let alone a snoopy cop in some distant town) would suspect anything amiss. The sanitised version is kept for the record or, better still, for exhibition in some select urban theatres to prove that everything is above board.

There is yet another way to frustrate the intentions of the govern-ment, and this is completely legit. Over the years, Hindi film-makers have perfected certain means of subterfuge to make a mockery of the censorship process and eventually have their way in celebrating sex on screen. They do this by making sure that one or more of the following elements are included in their films.

Mujra

The *Mujra* sequence is one of the oldest ploys of using feminine charm as a device for seduction, and much more. The dancer usually masquerades in a *kathak* costume, even as her mannerisms, gestures and steps are far removed from anything to do with any known folk or classical dance form. A bolder variation of this would be the cabaret, which is meant to serve the same purpose. A still further development on this is the risqué 'item number', with boys in tights and girls in bare nothings, serving more as an comic interlude than taking the narrative any further.

Holi Festivity

Holi festivity is a must since the seventies, with the hero entitled to take liberties with the heroine and molesting her on the pretext of applying colour and getting her drenched. In any other situation, the censors would have pounced on these scenes with their scissors, but here it is the divine Radha–Krishna myth being recreated, and even otherwise, as a courtship ritual the Holi revelry involving eligible young men and nubile girls enjoys social sanction. Quite often, the water pistol (pichkari) is brandished by an actor as a phallic symbol with crude, suggestive gestures and nobody can do anything about it.

Rape

A rape scene betrays another expression of bad taste but cannot be helped. So long as there are villains, there will be rape victims in films. Unlike the mandatory song and dance sequences, which do nothing to take a film forward, the rape scene, with its accompanying visuals of horror and depravity, becomes an important ingredient in the plot structure, very often triggering a turn in the course of events. In fact, there are many Hindi films that owe their success to an elaborate rape scene at the very beginning. The indignity notwithstanding, it is a good enough excuse to indulge in some skin show with the victim's clothes in disarray, her legs spread-eagled, injuries in her private parts and the villain in action with his pants down!

Tribal Rituals

In what other way can you get a line up of scantily dressed (even topless) women without raising the hackles of the censors than by including a sequence with tribals? Adorned with feathers and beads, they go about squawking and shrieking with their men folk in what has become Bollywood's standard representation of the aboriginal

way of life. Invariably, the hero finds himself in the midst (wilfully or accidentally) of this strange tribe, and after a good deal of breast-beating, song and dance and assorted mumbo-jumbo, he befriends them and together they set out to annihilate the villain.

Bridal Night

The bridal night scene is yet another time-honoured ruse to stir the viewer's baser instincts—the hero announcing his entry into the bridal chamber by shutting the door behind him, deliberately re-moving the garland around his neck and studying the woman, who, in all her bridal finery, is sitting on the bed with her head bowed, waiting for the man to make his first move. Everybody knows what happens next but never tire of seeing it enacted one more time. A film-maker will be failing in his duty if he is unable to oblige. That explains all the senseless tossing and turning we see of bridal couples on the bed, the furious groping and clutching between the sheets, and the asphyxiated grunts and groans. This is the kind of stuff audiences can never get enough of.

Mistaken Identity

Picture this. The hero accidentally bumps into the heroine in a rail coupe or at the airport. Together they fall, rolling over one another. Somehow, their suitcases get switched. The next scene: he opens her suitcase and screams as he holds aloft her bra. If that's not funny, imagine that he dresses up as an old man, or perhaps a fake doctor, or better still, another woman. He sidles up to the heroine, holds her hand in his and then feels her all over. Unsuspectingly, she lets him have his way till …. We have seen these scenes enacted by virtu-ally every hero, from Shammi Kapoor to Rishi Kapoor to Anil Kapoor and Govinda. And yet, we want more.

Lyrical Erotica

Lyrical erotica is less of a visual prank, although there have been instances like Mithun Chakraborty and Ayesha Julka enacting the infamous *kabootar* number in all its lurid detail. A later example would

be the *khatiya* song Govinda and Karishma Kapoor had performed in *Raja Babu* (1994). But in its most suggestive form think of all those *purdah* songs in which the hero unambiguously refers to the veil of the heroine as indicative of her virginity. You can't get any crasser than that.

◼ *Borderless Crime*

As though the Copyright Act and the Cinematograph Act were not enough, there are three more laws that the government can conveniently rely upon (should one or the other fail in a prosecution) in order to tighten its stranglehold on the film industry:

- Indian Penal Code (IPC), 1860
- Young Person's (Harmful) Publication Act (YPHPA), 1956
- Indecent Representation of Women Act (IRWA), 1986

Essentially, these are laws meant to put a check on the filming, exhibition and transmission of obscene and indecent images across all conceivable media. A subtle distinction is, however, made between the two operative words, 'obscene' and 'indecent'. Obscene material is defined as that which has the tendency to 'deprave those whose minds are open to immoral influences and into whose hands the material may fall'. Indecency has a slightly broader perspective and includes that which is 'obscene as well as representations that are derogatory or denigrating towards women'. Indecency is a far more serious crime than obscenity, with pornography falling somewhere between the two. While courts have held that pornography is an 'aggravated form of obscenity', opinion is divided on images or representations that may (or may not) be intended to arouse the baser instincts of audiences. A critical analysis of how these three articles of legislation operate in respect of the film industry would be in order:

Indian Penal Code

The IPC prohibits the 'sale, letting out on hire, public exhibition and in any other manner, circulating obscene material as well as the creation, import and export of and possession of such material' for the said purposes. It also seeks to outlaw profit-making and advertising of any business engaged in such objectionable activities. Its application to Internet has, however, given rise to some grave anomalies. This is because when the IPC was drafted, the world-wide web was nowhere on the scene. In effect, today, an intermediary unaware of the nature of images being transmitted (distributed or put into circulation) becomes technically open to prosecution, according to the provisions of the Act. Worse, a search engine which provides the service of searching for audio and visual content of a film on the Internet becomes criminally liable even as the representation could be a mere automated copy of a doctored or morphed image resident in some other non-affiliated website. Websites on which people are allowed to upload pictures could be exposing themselves all the more to liability under the IPC as they have no control over what a consumer might choose to upload. In most cases, the website would not be uploading the visuals, but by virtue of distributing the same, it makes itself liable. Such are the dangers of dealing with a supremely vibrant and interactive medium like the Internet.

Young Person's (Harmful) Publication Act (YPHPA)

The YPHPA provides for penalties similar to those of the IPC, only that its purview is limited to persons below the age of 20 years. But the expression 'harmful publication' is usually interpreted by the courts in the widest possible sense and includes both obscene and indecent material which can have a damaging effect on young, impressionable minds. As such, the anomalies in the application of the Act to cyberspace become much sharper than those concerning the IPC. With the Internet reaching out to more and more youngsters, the unique nature of the medium and the possibilities that it unfolds have exposed the limitations of the Act even more, thereby forcing lawmakers to do a rethink about its relevance.

Indecent Representation of Women Act (IRWA)

The IRWA prohibits the publication, sending by post and transmission of material that amounts to compromising the dignity of women. Advertisements of a similar nature are also banned by the Act. But again, it can do little to contain such offences particularly when these are generated and transmitted by the Internet advertising industry. A peculiarity of this industry is that advertisements featured on websites are frequently controlled by people other than the one who owns the website. The nature of control is such that it extends to even manipulating or altering the advertisement without the knowledge of the owner of the website. By imposing liabilities on an entity publishing or participating in an advertisement, the statute may well be rendering all such operations on the Internet both commercially and legally untenable.

A far graver risk that emerges from these Acts is that innocent persons could easily be framed, and even arrested, strictly by following the letter of the law. The principles of traditional jurisprudence governing conditions for arrest and presentation of evidence in court hold no relevance whatsoever in matters relating to cyber crimes. This became startlingly clear in late 2004 when the owner of an auction website was arrested by the Mumbai police for no apparent fault of his. Somebody had visited his site and put up on sale an obscene multi-media clip he had no knowledge of, let alone have anything to do with. But in his capacity as an Internet Service Provider (ISP), the burden of proving non-culpability fell on him and till such time as he could do so, he was presumed guilty and denied bail by the courts. Such are the hidden dangers of juggling with laws between the real and virtual worlds.

Now, there is also the Information Technology (IT) Act of 2000 which is supposed to take care of these anomalies. It categorically attaches criminal liability to 'any person who publishes, transmits or causes to publish any obscene material' on the Net, while absolving a service provider of any blame if he automatically transmits obscene material he has no knowledge of. But before he can seek

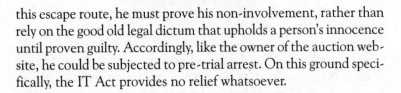

this escape route, he must prove his non-involvement, rather than rely on the good old legal dictum that upholds a person's innocence until proven guilty. Accordingly, like the owner of the auction website, he could be subjected to pre-trial arrest. On this ground specifically, the IT Act provides no relief whatsoever.

These are some very real issues concerning all film-makers hosting websites as part of their marketing strategy and pre-release publicity campaigns. They all recognise the potential of the Internet in furthering business and some could even be considering the production of Net films (especially after *This is Not a Love Story*, the first movie to be officially launched on the Internet in 2003), only that nobody is sure about the ground they could be treading on. One false step and anybody could find himself behind bars. So long as the government persists with the haphazard enforcement of an uncertain legal regime, such confusion will prevail in public minds. The obvious way out would be for law enforcement agencies to turn a blind eye to all transgressions on the obscenity and indecency counts. But that would be an unbelievably simplistic, even if a practical solution for the government to even consider.

For all its advantages, the biggest problem with the Internet is its borderless nature. It is the only mass medium known to mankind that is completely global. Should you want to host a website tomorrow (if you have not already done so), which law would you comply with? For example, if your server is located in the U.S. and caters to South African customers and is accessible from any part of the world (including India), the laws of which country do you abide by? What is permissible in the U.S. could well be unacceptable in India, and vice versa. And what is banned in South Africa could be a non-issue elsewhere in the world. How do you then streamline such a disparate situation? In the absence of a uniform legal regime, or at least an international convention on issues relating to jurisdiction and choice of law on the Internet, confusion is bound to prevail in all quarters.

To an extent, the U.K. has resolved this issue by indicating (albeit stupidly) that transmission of data to an ISP and from there to a

viewer's computer are acts amounting to 'publication' under its Obscene Publications Act of 1959. Therefore, even if a server is not located in the U.K. but the offending material is downloaded there, it would be punishable by the Act. This approach seems to be shared by most governments across the globe, whereby the content of a website, and not its location, becomes the incriminating factor in the eyes of law. Indian lawmakers are moving in this direction, little realising how absurd such legislation can turn out to be. The government will then expect entertainment companies (including film production houses) to conform to the near impossibility of publishing only such material on the Internet that conforms to the obscenity laws of every single country in the world. What needs to be understood here is that obscenity and indecency are just notional concepts of public propriety and cannot be subjected to definitions of law anywhere.

Content Regulation

These are just a few obvious examples of how the state gets to exercise its control on the creation, exhibition and transmission of content on the Internet and elsewhere. Any alert film-maker would know that there are many other and more subtle ways for the government to ensure that its control on the industry is complete. Ultimately, he must function only at the pleasure of the government, regardless of how he interprets his 'fundamental right' to freedom of expression in a so-called progressive democracy. He may not realise this as much at the production stage as when his prints are out of the lab and his cans are put up for distribution. It is then that he is confronted with a bewildering range of choices. He must decide on scheduling the release in theatres, sale of overseas and satellite rights, distributing video clippings and songs to broadcasting organisations, tapping the home video circuit, mobile telephone companies and broadband (high speed Internet) services, including the cable network. All these possibilities, which were non-existent till the other day, are available now, thanks to the prevailing media boom and merging of market structures. But with the government intent upon playing spoil sport, the film-maker knows that he cannot just avail of all the facilities and must selectively adopt the line of least contention in exercising his choices. To an extent, he is also guided by the content of his film.

On its part, the government recognises that there is no way progress in technology can be stopped and, with every passing day, content will become easier and cheaper for the masses to access. Moreover, as the lines defining various markets in the media get blurred, the good old laws like the IPC, Copyright Act, IRWA, YPHPA and Cinematograph Act will soon become redundant. So there is talk of newer laws, such as, the Broadcasting Act (which seeks to set up the Broadcasting Authority of India or BAI) and Convergence Act which will regulate the 'different kinds of services over the existing infrastructure and the enhancement of existing technologies to provide a wider variety of services'. Also on the cards is a Communications Commission of India (CCI) which shall serve as a super-regulator for telecom, broadcasting and information technology services. Furthermore, there would be a Spectrum Management Committee empowered to issue licenses and adjudicate disputes.

However sugar-coated the government's proclamations on the subject may be, it cannot disguise its anxiety to tighten its hold on the marketplace and create further confusion all around. Already there are two regulatory bodies functioning under the communications ministry—department of telecommunications (DoT) and the Telecom Regulatory Authority of India (TRAI). All they have succeeded in doing so far is sedulously interfere with the free flow of market forces and thwart the growth and accessibility of communications technology in the country. But then, nothing can be done. As they say, the path to hell is paved with noble intentions. One such declared intention is to 'facilitate and regulate all matters relating to content and to specify codes and standards in relation to the same'. Accordingly, publishing and sending of obscene or

offensive messages will be punishable with imprisonment up to three years or with fine up to Rs 20 million or both.

The proposed Communications Commission is supposed to ensure that every service provider of content application will 'endeavour to provide a suitable proportion' of programmes of indigenous origin and inter-alia perform the following two key functions:

1. Take steps to regulate or curtail harmful and illegal content on the Internet and other communication services.

2. Specify codes and standards to ensure fairness and impartiality in the presentation of content and ensure emphasis on promotion of Indian culture, values of national integration, religious and communal harmony and scientific temper.

Expressions such as 'harmful and illegal content', 'fairness and impartiality', 'Indian culture' and 'suitable proportion' have not been defined and, therefore, are open to subjective interpretation. Furthermore, the proposed legislation on media convergence prescribes severe penalties to any person who sends 'by means of a communication service or a network infrastructure any content that he knows to be false and persistently makes use of that content to cause annoyance, inconvenience or needless anxiety to another'. Once again, no standards have been specified to determine the scope of application of offence. Words like 'annoyance', 'inconvenience' and 'needless anxiety' are so vague that they only invite arbitrariness in enforcement.

While communication experts are grappling with these issues, what has escaped public attention is the original source of inspiration for the proposed instruments of legislation. One was Malaysia, where the Communication and Multi-media Act stipulates that 'no content applications service provider shall provide content which is indecent, obscene, false, menacing or offensive in character with intent to annoy, abuse, threaten or harass any person'. The other relevant source of inspiration is the U.K., where, under the Communications Act of 2003, the Office of Communications (OFCOM) takes care

of 'matters that concern the contents of anything, which is or may be broadcast or otherwise transmitted by means of electronic communications networks' and 'the promotion of public understanding or awareness of matters relating to the publication of matter by means of the electronic media'. No ambiguous terms or standards are mentioned, though at one point, the Act mentions that OFCOM is entrusted with the duty of promoting media literacy and revising, from time to time, a standards code.

Significantly, in the cases of both Malaysia and the U.K., a single convergent regulator has been entrusted with the powers of content regulation. Also, whether it is the OFCOM or the Malaysian Commission of Communication and Multi-media (MCCM), the mechanism of regulation is decentralised with content providers as well as content viewers encouraged to *participate* in the decision-making and enforcement processes. Unlike in India, the flow of power is not unidirectional, from top to bottom. This is in clear recognition of the fact that with developments in technology, content of media and communication have become easily accessible through various means and, thus, it is impossible for a single regulator, located in the national capital, to regulate the content viewed by masses across the country.

In a vast country like India, a decentralised structure becomes all the more necessary if any regulation has to work. Moreover, it has to be a participative process with industry representatives being taken into confidence. Consequently, in 2005, the Confederation of Indian Industries (CII) had petitioned the government with a four-point programme to modify the content regulation mechanism in the country:

1. There should be a mechanism for regulation of content and decision making at the local level. For this purpose, steps should be taken to increase public awareness with respect to the regulatory measures and to encourage media literacy.

2. In addition to the functions of content regulation entrusted on the convergence regulator, the industry should be encouraged

to develop its own codes and standards to regulate content and to comply with the same. These industry codes should be submitted to the regulatory body for review.

3. Additionally, the content/service providers may be required to have internal checks to ensure the quality of content viewed by the public. Such internal bodies may be required to submit periodical reports to the single convergence authority.

4. Finally, the approach towards content regulation should be flexible and responsive towards the present society's perception of acceptable standards for content.

For Bollywood film-makers, two basic facts emerge from these developments. The first is that the CII, as indeed all content and service providers in India, are reconciled to the fact that the media cannot be extricated from the clutches of the government. One way or the other, it will find a pretext to regulate content and the Constitution be damned. The time-honoured explanation that no freedom is absolute and must be necessarily accompanied by appropriate checks and balances will hold good in this case too. The second disturbing fact is that Bollywood has absolutely no voice to influence the decisions affecting it, even as there is the Film Federation of India (FFI) on paper to take care of its interests. Today, its role and authority have been hijacked by bodies like the FICCI and CII, leaving the industry with no choice but to rely on their good offices in all its representations to the government. The past few years have revealed that both FICCI and CII have far more pressing issues to lobby for in the government than even bother with entertainment. Bollywood, in any case, is the least of its concerns.

eight

Rise of Consuming Classes

Whatever may be said about government controls, one fact remains eminently clear—India is currently at the cusp of an unprecedented media boom. With newer content providers showing up every other day, there can be no stopping the nation from emerging as a leading global player for promoting the exchange of information products, but for one inhibiting factor. And that has nothing to do with state intervention. Sooner than later, the dynamics of free trade will come into play, whereby smaller content providers will find it impossible to sustain themselves and shall be weeded out one way or the other. After this market shake-out, the larger players will inevitably consolidate their positions and the industry will reach a state of maturity. Here, in a stable environment, it will not be quantity but the quality of content—with an accent on innovation and creativity—that shall drive the Indian mass media.

Clearly, the nation is not very far from reaching that stage of stability. The indicators are already there. Since the early nineties, government emphasis on economic reforms has created a healthy environment for foreign investments and ensured a steady growth of the GDP beyond the benchmark of 8 per cent. Today, India ranks among the top five economies of the world in terms of purchasing power parity and according to the estimates of leading global investors it is only a matter of time before India overtakes China as the fastest growing entertainment industry. This is primarily due to its 300 million-strong middle class population who is increasingly allocating a

higher percentage of its disposable income on entertainment products. Rising consumerism in this section of the population is evident from the following economic indicators:

- Automobile sales are rising steadily every year. In two-wheeler sales, India ranks second in the world, while car sales are over a million per annum and growing at a blistering rate of 25 per cent.

- India is the sixth largest market for mobile handsets (16 million units per annum) and is growing at 50 per cent per annum.

- The country is the fifth largest market for colour television sets and is growing at a consistent 25 per cent per annum.

Consumption spending is directly related to increasing disposable incomes on account of sustained growth in income levels and reductions in personal income tax since the mid-nineties. Consequent changes in lifestyle have led to companies allocating higher budgets for the advertising and marketing of discretionary products and services. Increased investments in such promotional activities automatically provide a boost to the entertainment industry for further growth. In fact, it has been observed across the world that this cyclically sensitive industry grows faster than the GDP when the economy expands. And lest this be viewed as a phenomenon benefiting the urban nouveau riche, here are some more economic pointers:

- Rural India has around 42,000 *haats* (including weekend markets) where consumer durables are bought and sold.

- In 2002–2003, 50 per cent of the policies sold by the state-owned Life Insurance Corporation (LIC) across India were in villages.

- Small towns and villages accounted for 1.3 million cellular telephone users in 2006.

- Of the 25 million households that purchased television sets between 2001 and 2004, 19 million (or 77 per cent) were from the rural hinterlands.

- Of the 20 million new subscriptions to a popular horizontal portal (providing e-commerce and free e-mail service) in 2004,

60 per cent were from small towns and villages. And of the 100,000-odd persons who had transacted on the shopping site, over 52,000 were again from India's small towns and villages.

In 2005–2006, the Indian rural market accounted for an estimated 128 million households, nearly three times that of urban India. This has been a huge opportunity going abegging, largely due to reasons of poor connectivity and logistics. Fuelled by good monsoons and an increase in agricultural output, symbols of affluence are showing up all around. Today, rural India boasts of over 40 per cent of India's middle class and over 50 per cent of the nation's total disposable income. Companies and businesses are recognising the potential of this consuming class and have accordingly managed to differentially cater to the varying segments. Their prosperity holds valuable lessons both for multinationals eyeing the Indian market and for the domestic entertainment industry. They all realise that the secret to gaining a competitive edge in the Indian marketplace lies in offering a broad spectrum of products and services aimed at specific segments, e.g., television channels for children. Without a focused, proactive and sustained targeting of niche segments, they could easily be lost in a crowd and will eventually suffer from a loss of identity.

Another significant factor that has led to the rise in consumerism is the fact that the average Indian spender is getting younger. Not only does he show a greater propensity to indulge and entertain himself, he has the means to do so as well. He marries late, is better informed and, above all, capable of earning more than his father and uncles did at a comparable age. The quantum of disposable income at his command is also much, much higher. Increased life expectancy, education, exposure to the media and a booming economy have together made this possible. Never before has the nation's youth played a more decisive role in determining the fortunes of companies dealing in anything from specialty food and fashion wear to travel and tourism, cell phones, home video systems, perfume and beauty products. As KSA-Technopak, an Indian retail consultancy noted in 2004:

Because of India's status as a good IT hub for outsourcing by U.S. companies, young Indians between 20 and 24 years, who ordinarily would not be able to find work easily, are securing jobs with call centres straight out of college. This is a consumer base that typically lives at home with the family. Their essentials have already been taken care of. So much of what they earn is disposable income.

It is almost entirely discretionary and, significantly, about 20 to 30 per cent higher than prevailing wages in other industries. This money is being channelised into huge spending on books, movies, music, cell phones, food and branded clothes. From the point of view of elders in the family, these are not strictly essentials and could even be considered luxuries. But the fact that demand for such non-essentials is continually rising explains why it makes more sense for advertisers of discretionary products to target the youth (and even kids), rather than the older generation. This spirit of youth is being reflected in the content and treatment of Bollywood cinema as well.

Yet another factor influencing the changing complexion of the entertainment industry is the rising numbers of Indians settled abroad. At present, over 20 million migrants in different parts of the globe are pushing the demand for India-oriented entertainment, be it films, television, video, music cassettes, CDs or live shows. As accessibility to these products increases, the orientation of producers of such entertainment undergoes a transformation. Already, catering to the local populace has become second priority to most content producers, as their goal today is to earn in dollars, euros and pounds, rather than in rupees. The most successful film-makers are those who command a loyal following outside the nation's boundaries. And since Bollywood cinema is primarily personality-driven, films written around stars like Shahrukh Khan, Amitabh Bachchan, Aishwarya Rai and others who enjoy a huge fan following abroad can never run at a loss. Even when a Shahrukh Khan-starrer like *Swades* (2004) or *Paheli* (2005) bombs in India, producers are assured of making up for their losses from the overseas market. That is what being Indian and thinking global does.

A distinction must, however, be made between cinema and the other media on which the growth of the film industry is dependent. Print, radio, television, etc., do not depend so much on subscriptions as films do, since they are driven to a large extent by sponsors or advertisers. Consequently, the rising affluence of consumers has no direct impact on them. An increase in marginal savings or dispos-able income rarely changes a person's reading or television viewing habit, but it certainly influences his affordability and, in effect, the frequency of his purchasing cinema tickets. Of course, rising con-sumerism does inspire advertisers to invest in entertainment channels and, in turn, influence consumer behaviour towards the products and services promoted. It is from this ad-spend that the non-film entertainment media draws its sustenance—at least, till such time as they are not completely subscription-driven.

Happily, ad-spends on the entertainment industry have been growing at a healthy 10 to 13 per cent every year since 2001. In relation to the GDP though, the ratio is less than 1 per cent—among the lowest in the world. In 2004, for instance, ad-spend for India stood at 0.5 per cent of the GDP as against 1.0 per cent in Australia, 1.3 per cent in the U.S. and 2.1 per cent in Hong Kong. For China, it was 0.6 per cent. In most industrialised economies, ad-spends hover around the region of 1 per cent of the GDP, which is generally regarded as the international norm. India could take some time reaching that level, but the fact that it hasn't as yet, underscores the potential that has been left untapped. Given the increasing number of media channels that consumers are being ex-posed to, brands will necessarily have to advertise more frequently and across more channels to generate brand recall. The biggest beneficiary of this activity is most likely to be television.

Consumption Patterns

While cinema also stands (though indirectly) to benefit from this media explosion, one possible dampener would be an economic

downturn. So long as the economy continues to grow, advertising budgets will keep ballooning. The moment it hits a rough patch (say, due to a bad monsoon or a global adversity like war or a rise in oil prices), productivity of the expenses on advertisements will be challenged. Professionally run companies are already asking their ad agencies to link their fees to performance indicators, such as, sales growth and added revenues. Film producers too are raising addressability issues with their publicists and putting to test the efficacy of every medium of communication. Advertising and publicity agents can no longer get away with promising the moon while acquiring an account and not delivering later.

In such a competitive scenario, two factors assume great importance. The first relates to content—the fact that there is no room for any compromise on quality and that poor, sub-standard work, whether in films, radio, television or music, will inevitably be rejected by the consumer. The second important factor is the extent of maturity reached by different sectors of the Indian entertainment industry. Every advertiser and publicist has to take into account both these factors before tailoring his promotional strategy to the available budget.

Cinema, of course, is regarded as the most mature of all the entertainment sectors. With a legacy of close to a century and an output of nearly 1,000 films a year, Indian cinema has reached a phase where the focus must necessarily be on the quality of content. In terms of maturity of internal processes also—the ability to attract investments and skilled personnel, the extent of competition in distribution and so on—cinema is streets ahead of television, radio, music and other sectors. But then, commercial success has never been directly proportionate to increase in the number of films, thereby compelling production houses to cut down on quality and make compromises at different levels. This is an unfortunate ground reality. The situation is such that, today, unless Indian film-makers take to advanced production techniques with visual flourishes, special effects, sound sync and so on, they will not be able to draw full advantage of their potential and, eventually, lose their critical advantage to the West.

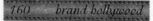

The same cannot be said about television though. It is still at an early stage of growth, even as channels devoted to entertainment, education and children's programming have reached an appreciable level of maturity. In fact, different genres are at different stages of their life cycle within the television medium. The news channels are believed to be next in the stage of evolution and, with the introduction of newer distribution modes such as DTH (direct-to-home) and IP-TV (internet protocol television), the demand for premium or alternate content, such as, teenage entertainment and adult programmes (subject to a liberalisation of the programming code) will also increase. Similarly, in music and radio, the emergence of newer players has led to a spurt in content availability, and genres like Indipop, devotionals and other forms of non-film music are gradually gaining in popularity. Simultaneously, technology has facilitated easy access to music through illegal downloads, pirated CDs and tapes, music television channels and even radio FM stations. Consequently, there has been little value realisation from experimentation and, with minimal support from the government, music companies are hardly able to make ends meet. Experts believe that with the rising popularity of non-film music, the situation will only change for the better. In any event, things cannot get any worse from here.

Film production houses and broadcasters are naturally concerned about the drop in the quality of music being produced and have been trying to revive the golden era of film music of the fifties and sixties. Their tacit support to remixes and cover versions of yesteryears' hits is part of that effort. But there is a pricing element to be considered as well. The price of music production is significantly lower in India than in other parts of the world, which goes well with the country's low per capita level of income. It also makes India an attractive destination for international production houses and broadcasters, who could always fall back on the large population base for high volume consumption. This, however, is true only in theory. In practice, access to volumes is restricted by fragmentation in the distribution chain. Added to this is the scourge of illegal downloads and unauthorised cassettes and CDs hitting the market with unfailing regularity. Somebody has to pay the price for these revenue leakages and this is reflected in the unrealistic price tags. Far from the issue getting resolved, music companies have been sent on a tailspin, with the incidence of piracy and revenue leakages mounting.

Oddly enough, this story is common to all sectors of the entertainment industry. In television, for instance, leakages are caused through low subscriber declarations by cable distributors. (According to an independent research, the operator-broadcaster split of subscription revenue in India is the worst skew in the world.) Similarly, in films leakages are caused by under-declaration of box-office receipts, mainly to evade entertainment tax. This is particularly true of small towns where not even the receipts of the biggest all-India hits are accounted for. (Significantly, many such theatres in Uttar Pradesh and Bihar are owned by political bigwigs, police officers and senior bureaucrats.) The total revenue Bollywood loses due to unaccounted receipts, coupled with video piracy, is estimated to be between Rs 15 and Rs 20 billion annually. Film piracy through DVD and VCD releases and the clandestine screening of new releases by cable channels are forcing film producers to pre-sell television and video rights (even before the film's release in theatres), thereby leading to further erosion in box-office revenues.

Now how do you reconcile this financial drag with the rise in consumerism? On the one hand, India is witnessing an unprecedented improvement in income levels across a large section of the population with a significant number of 18 to 35-year-olds both willing and capable to spend on entertainment. On the other hand, the internal dynamics of various segments of the industry, revenue leakages and unrealistic pricing have together conspired to deny content creators their just dues. From the industry perspective, the situation is much like the predicament of the proverbial monkey on a slippery pole who moves three steps up and two steps down. To make matters worse, there still exists a substantive difference in affordability levels between every section of Indian society. No matter what media analysts have to say, the fact is that there remains a huge percentage of Indians who still go hungry to bed every night and for whom entertainment holds little or no meaning. To the industry, they are completely invisible. Their existence is not recognised, simply because they have no contribution to make in revenue generation.

In the circumstances, the more clever corporate tacticians have learnt to adopt a differential pricing strategy based on the income levels of consumers and their geographical spread. Broadly, this follows the good old Marxist principle that the affluent should subsidise the poor. It is a ruse to optimise revenues from the same product or service. So personality and behavioural traits are taken into account to not only monitor, but also pre-determine and, wherever possible, manipulate responses to promotional messages from select target groups. The elements of consumer character make for what is understood as a psychographic profile. According to the *Consumer Outlook Survey* of 2005 (published by KSA-Technopak), four distinct psychographic profiles can be identified at an all-India level for entertainment products: the comfortably affluent (comprising 26.9 per cent of the population), the first adopters (consisting of 36.3 per cent), the social emulators (20.3 per cent) and the indifferent sceptics (16.5 per cent).

The segregation leads to some interesting observations on consumer behaviour at a geographical level. For instance, those living in northern India (particularly Delhi and Ludhiana) are predominantly driven by a herd mentality and, as social emulators, are constantly trying to keep up with the Joneses. They are more conformists than individualistic or trendsetters. In contrast, southern India has the highest number of first adopters, thanks largely to the three metros—Bangalore, Chennai and Hyderabad. Acceptance of new technology and gadgets, hi-fashion wear, lifestyle and entertainment products is the highest in the South as compared to the rest of the country. Eastern India is dominated by the indifferent sceptics who are the slowest at adopting the latest in fashion and technology. They are least influenced by peer pressure, advertisements or celebrity persuasion as they remain socially more inward in their attitude and consumption. Finally there are the comfortably affluent, who

are evenly distributed across the country—the most prominent being in the West and South.

Furthermore, the study revealed that the first adopter is psychologically more avant-garde and forward looking than those in the other segments. He is most influenced by the celebrities he admires, is fairly conscious of the image he projects, is particular about the clothes and gadgets he purchases, is prone to experimentation, individualistic and a trendsetter in his own way. He is the polar opposite of the indifferent sceptic who is not in sync with fashion and latest products. Slow to adopt technology and gizmos, the latter is less aware of global trends and, strangely enough, averse to taking loans for lifestyle products. He is typically the oldest in age of the four segments and spends only as much as he can comfortably afford.

Significantly, the comfortably affluent consumer also presents a picture in sharp contrast to the first adopter. The most distinctive trait of this group is that it is the least price sensitive of the four segments. The comfortably affluent is also average on the other parameters of early adoption, being individualistic and influenced by peers or advertisements, but he accounts for the highest spends, particularly on domestic appliances, furniture and home textiles. In comparison, the social emulator betrays strong herd mentality, is not very individualistic and can easily be influenced by peers.

The unorganised cable operators of the television sector were among the first to recognise the advantages of differential pricing pegged to the psychographic profile of consumers. Establishment of zones and accordingly creating a zonal pricing structure for different cable subscription packages have now become the industrial norm. So, for the service you receive on television in, say, Mumbai or Delhi, your monthly cable charges are far higher than what people in Kolkata or Kanpur pay. Within Mumbai itself, a vast difference exists between what a slum dweller in Govandi pays and what is charged from residents of a tony Lokhandwala high rise. This way, the revenue from higher income groups subsidises the service to lower income groups (with scarcely a difference in content packages) and, in the bargain, the subscription base gets to be expanded. More importantly, through this differential pricing, barriers are erected against the infiltration of competitors and revenues are thus maximised.

In films, differential pricing has existed since the birth of Bollywood, both at the distribution (geographical territories) and exhibition (theatre hall tickets) levels. With the proliferation of multiplexes and the tax holidays announced by state governments for promoting their growth, price differentials have now come under close scrutiny. Exhibitors are engaging market researchers to gain a thorough understanding of the price sensitivities of various segments and ensuring equitable distribution of value. The idea, very clearly, is to determine optimal ticketing rates in each segment that will not only draw larger audiences to films but also maximise revenue. It is not enough to have a full house if the paying capacity of audiences is not fully exploited. So red carpets, plush sofas and such frills are introduced in cinema halls for the benefit of those who can afford and are paying for these special privileges. In a strange way, the community of black market touts can serve as a reliable market barometer for gauging the true value of the paying public. Exhibitors who shut their eyes to this reality are only exposing themselves to more revenue leakages.

Technology Effects

Closely related to pricing is the influence of technology on the entertainment industry. Continual technological upgradation not only ensures the raising of industry standards, but also redefines products, cost structure and distribution. Even the thinking of content creators changes accordingly. For instance, in 1940, barely eight years after sound entered Indian cinema, Mehboob Khan made *Aurat* with Sardar Akhtar. Seventeen years later, in 1957, he made the same film with Nargis in the lead and called it *Mother India*, which

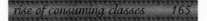

turned into an all-time classic. More than his heroine, it was the availability of better filming equipment (indeed, cameras and recorders) that prompted the production of the revised version. Today, as remakes of yesteryears' hits like *Devdas* (2002), *Parineeta* (2005) and *Don* (2006) hit the screen, the same logic holds good. The storyline remains the same, but technology has changed and, hence, the treatment has changed. Barring the title which holds a recall value for the audience, the experience is often akin to watching a completely different movie. The good thing is that the box-office is responding favourably to such repeats.

The biggest impact of technology has been in the areas of sound recording, visual effects and animation. In television, the growing adoption of digital technology has enhanced the experience of content viewing and listening even more. Leading global broadcasting companies are now placing development and the use of new technologies at the centre of their core marketing strategies. For other content distributors also, the emerging picture is very clear. Their survival will depend solely on the ability to embrace technology and, in effect, offer increasingly superior services—high-resolution pictures, high-speed Internet access, online games and information, satellite radio, pay-per-view electronic commerce services, voice telephony, etc. Technology typically reduces the price per contact and raises initial capital expenditure. In the circumstances, the only hope left for content providers is to set off the hike in costs against the possibility of extended market reach and incremental volume gains. This element of uncertainty has to be evaluated every time an investment in technology is made.

Today, the technological options open to entertainment companies are as momentous as they are far reaching. Some of them have already been discussed in previous chapters, but they would bear repetition if certain significant trends in media distribution are to be tracked and the manner these would impact entertainment consumption in times to come:

Digitisation

Both television and cinema are heading towards an era of total digitisation of content—not because the facility already exists and that it helps in producing sharper images and better sound quality on screen. Going digital is the smartest thing to do if TV channels and film producers are serious about plugging leakages in last-mile revenues. Everybody knows that there is just no way to compel cable operators and theatre owners to make an honest declaration of their collections.

High Definition Television (HDTV)

As digital video signals become the norm, prices of HDTV sets are expected to drop significantly. As of now though, sales of current-generation television sets have shown no indication of a slump. In fact, consumers are continuing to pay more for large screen models with the old, trusted technology. Even in the West, viewers have not switched to HDTV sets because of the high price differential.

Digital Audio

As technology enables Internet users to download digital audio tracks, online music download sites will proliferate and pose a challenge to conventional music companies and radio stations. Nowadays, artistes are opting more often for launching their albums online rather than taking the more expensive and cumbersome music video or radio station route. In fact, recording companies are also moving towards offering their music online. Digital distribution is a means for both artistes and producers to bypass radio stations and tele-vision music channels.

Personal Video Recorder (PVR)

The PVR expands users' ability to decide when and how television programmes are to be watched. It allows the viewer to pause a pro-gramme when required and, more importantly, the luxury to skip commercials entirely. Effectively, the PVR enables viewers to create their own programming schedules to fit into their leisure hours.

The flip side of such technology is that it will lead to more audience fragmentation. Television companies unable to provide suitable programming content will be driven out of the market, sooner than later.

Interactive Services

Digital broadcasters are working on ways and means to include interactive services into their over-the-air digital video transmissions, primarily as video signal enhancements. Cable and satellite companies are also moving towards interactive services that vary from simple video-on-demand to more complex Internet access products. Such interactive technologies are expected to be platform-neutral, enabling service providers to offer newer products and services by the day.

Fixed Broadband Wireless

This is another way of bringing interactive digital services to consumers. These are still early days in figuring out the commercial pros and cons of the use of point-to-point, as against point-to-multipoint technology. The point-to-point facility involves beaming of data over the air from a transmitter to one receiver. The technology is already well-entrenched in parts of Asia, though mainly for business-to-business communication. Point-to-multipoint, in comparison, is still at its embryonic stage and operates much like satellite distribution, beaming data to as many reception antennae as the signals can reach. The day is not far when movie releases will take this form of a satellite shower.

Internet Radio

With speedy Internet access and easy availability of sophisticated software, music lovers will benefit tremendously in the future. Free downloadable audio players for computers have already raised the quality of listening experience. Traditional over-the-air radio stations are now exploiting the Internet's ability to deliver audio clips along with graphics, data and video at the same time. The Internet has also extended the reach of radio stations beyond

traditional markets (which was determined by the strength of their broadcast signals) to the entire world.

Satellite Radio

This is a digital radio broadcast system that uses direct-to-home satellite technology to offer listeners up to 100 channels of commercial-free audio music, news and entertainment. In July 2005, World Space Asia made its India debut with what it claimed as the 'King of Radio', offering 39 dedicated stations, 24 hours a day. Though public response was initially lukewarm, the announcement was seen as a precursor of the possibilities about to unfold.

Significantly, it is not as though all the new technologies are meant to succeed. India is known to be an extremely price-sensitive market. For any technology to therefore find mass acceptance, it is imperative that it adds value both for the consumers and service providers. This is a tall order. Besides, the gradual penetration of digital connectivity and the support of quality infrastructure are factors that cannot be overlooked. Furthermore, new emerging technologies are bound to have a disruptive effect (though temporarily) on the business models of media and entertainment companies, thereby upsetting the existing industry equilibrium from time to time. Film producers would have to take all these variables into account before drawing up strategies for delivery in the future.

■ Big Picture

As of now though, Bollywood can only be expected to wait and watch. Even as cinema is an important component of the entertainment industry, it is pointless for film-makers to intervene in the ongoing churning process. They are in no position to directly influence the forces of consumerism, differential pricing and technological breakthroughs. In that respect, they will have to remain at the receiving end. But it is crucial that they are also aware of the direction in

which the winds of change are blowing and, accordingly, gear themselves towards all possible eventualities. Ultimately, there are two inescapable facts they will be compelled to contend with: (*i*) having to tailor their films according to the delivery platforms shaped by technology and (*ii*) having to better themselves progressively in quality, as there is no space for mediocre content any longer.

An overview of the Hindi film industry will reveal that the extent of value destruction caused by medium-budget films (between Rs 100 and 200 million) is as high as 90 per cent. For reasons ranging from poor scripting and unplanned production to a pronounced lack of process orientation and financial indiscipline, these films did not stand a ghost of a chance at the box-office. And yet, they continue to be made. If statistics is any indicator, what needs to be understood is that the chances of success rise significantly the moment a film is budgeted under Rs 100 million, in which case, the period for recouping costs is reduced. Alternatively, a film has to be considerably over-budgeted to provide for not only saleable stars and high production values, but also media partners and promotions, marketing and the simultaneous release of multiple prints. But then, Bollywood film-makers are committing the blunder of choosing the middle-path with medium-budgets and middling stars (in the mistaken belief of playing safe), only to find themselves saddled with a mediocre film and no takers. Such regressive practices have led to value destruction, hampering intervention of positive change and, in the long run, slowing down the growth of the film industry.

Linear growth projections made by the so-called film pundits often ignore these ground realities and betray limited understanding of the potential of the sector. Consider this:

- India's per capita adult-spend on films is less than Rs 2 a year. At a projected compounded annual growth rate (CAGR) of 20 per cent, this could at best rise to Rs 3 (taking population growth also into account) per person by the year 2010. This, however, does not represent the true potential of the film industry in a country of over a billion people. For most of them, cinematic entertainment is the sole leisure activity.

- With nearly 200 television channels and 48 million cable homes, India is the third largest cable economy in the world after the U.S. and China. But India also has the second lowest (after China) per capita cable-spend at Rs 150 per home per month. The hourly price realisation from a family of five per day per person with an average television viewing of one hour per day per person works out to be just Re 1. Considering that cable is still not reaching even one-fourth of India's 200 million households, it is clear that a projected CAGR of 20 per cent grossly understates the real potential of television.

Optimal utilisation of the potential of film and television will require fundamental sectoral changes including strategic and structural corrections, adoption of new technologies, improved consumer connect and organisational effectiveness. The fact remains that Indian consumers of entertainment are not waiting to be redefined and will sing and dance together to whatever, whenever the industry makes available. So any prediction about them exercising choices can only be presumptuous and will amount to placing the cart before the horse. Moreover, no matter what the product is, a consumer will respond to it on three fundamental counts: quality, convenience and price. There is no fourth factor he considers. If you've got two of these three factors right, you've won him over.

The evolutionary process followed by different sectors of the industry defines the need, nature and rationale of the changes that can be expected in the future. Cinema being the oldest and relatively most conservative sector of the industry, has responded reluctantly to every change, including the recent moves for corporatisation. Television, in contrast, is new and dynamic, enjoying huge investor confidence. Music falls somewhere in between. Home video, Internet, mobile telephony and others are comparatively fresh and untested. Consequently, the type and scale of issues faced by each differ from the rest of the industry segments. If one sector will require course correction, another might demand facilitative regulation, while a third could be asking for institutional intervention. The scale of these initiatives, degree of difficulty, relative importance,

complexity and level of risks will also vary from one sector to another. So drawing up a uniform organisational code to improve consumer connect for the Indian entertainment industry as a whole will be horribly gratuitous, if not facile.

What could, however, be explored is the possibility of unlocking value within each sector in keeping with the spirit of excellence. For this, leading industry players will have to rise above a state of complacency (which breeds inefficiencies) and (*i*) develop saleable products keeping in mind the socio-economic realities of the Indian market; (*ii*) improve operational effectiveness through global benchmarking, adoption of best practices as well as technology and strategic innovation; and (*iii*) leverage the capabilities developed so far in international markets. Once the leaders set the course, the rest of the industry will automatically fall in line.

In the past, industry leaders have got into so-called 'strategic alliances' with one another (or occasionally with a foreign player) for a variety of reasons—leveraging an enhanced market opportunity, better cost management, reducing revenue leakages, improving operational efficiency, developing deeper consumer insights and so on. But beyond fobbing off competition, such collaborative efforts have largely proved to be short-lived and no more than marriages of convenience. Far from contributing to the general growth of the industry, these alliances have created skewed market structures, characterised by several sectors remaining resource starved without management depth, organisational capabilities and administrative transparency. Oddly enough, parties to the alliance themselves fall into a trap of their own creation and the benefits are dissipated.

A case in point is the state-owned National Film Development Corporation (NFDC). In 1980, when it was flush with funds, it entered into a collaborative arrangement with Richard Attenborough for *Gandhi* on a 12 per cent profit sharing basis. Through the best part of the eighties, the 12 per cent returns from the film kept NFDC afloat as all its other projects, including independent film production and theatre construction, bombed. By the nineties, when revenue

from *Gandhi* petered out, NFDC was conclusively in the red. Despite government support, it could not raise itself from a state of complacency and compete with the private players in the market. Lack of managerial skills, reluctance to invest in systems and procedures as well as its inability to attract investments and talent, together resulted in its downfall.

Alliances of convenience do not last and cannot help anybody in the long run. This is all the more true in a changing competitive environment where newer, more organised and resourceful players are emerging every day. Significantly, most of these players are either off-shoots of corporate entities or, alternatively, have taken steps to transform themselves into corporate entities. Their business-like approach combined with alternative technologies and attractive value propositions on offer have greatly exposed the strategic vulnerability of traditional players insofar as the sustainability of profitable growth is concerned.

Furthermore, it must be understood that most crucial issues of the entertainment industry are closely interrelated and cut across the sectoral divide. Media convergence demands a holistic approach to the situation. Broadly, there are four major categories of common issues concerning every single content provider:

- Structural issues, including issues related to distribution of content down the value chain, extent of competition and level playing field.

- Revenue related issues emanate from the industry's inability to achieve and sustain growth rates commensurate with the industry potential.

- Profitability related issues resulting from a combination of the above two, along with an inability to manage costs.

- Resource related issues with regard to the industry's difficulties in attracting resources like investment and talent at reasonable costs.

Addressing these issues will amount to 'managing' the growth of each sector in relation to one another and, in effect, to the industry as a whole. We have trade bodies like the FFI (Film Federation of India) as well as FICCI (Federation of Indian Chambers of Commerce and Industry) and CII (Confederation of Indian Industries) which should have initiated the process by now, but beyond making periodic reviews of operating systems and strategies, nothing much seems to have come through in resolving any issue. The general explanation given is that solutions should come forth from industry players themselves and not be imposed by an external body. It is all very well and in keeping with the spirit of free will and democracy, only that, as Indians, we live by the belief, 'If it ain't broke, we won't fix it'! This attitude is reflected in the way businesses are conducted to this day throughout the country.

In the eyes of most Westerners, Indians are typically viewed as laid-back, fatalistic, yet argumentative. We have not been able to change that perception despite all our achievements in information technology, medicine, industry, academics, sports, and so on. In the field of entertainment, we are still seen as lazy copycats who would rather wait and watch than take the proverbial bull by its horns and turn opportunity into advantage. It would seem that a perpetual cash crunch, inequitable distribution of resources and government interventions have together made us pathologically more cautious than our Western counterparts into initiating changes. We are afraid to be the part of any change. This sense of caution is usually mis-interpreted as lack of enterprise, but should you put an Indian on a level playing field—especially on foreign soil—his survival instincts take over and he is bound to outdo all competition. This has been proved, time and again, by countless NRIs settled abroad and pursuing different vocations.

At home, complacency sets in the moment we find our comfort levels. This is human nature. We were happy witnesses to the first wave of growth in the entertainment sector following the opening up of the economy in the early nineties. We watched with amazement as the skies exploded with new television channels entering our homes, the Internet redefining our lives, and mobile telephony making communication so much simpler. All of a sudden, the world had shrunk and we actually felt part of a large global community.

Some of us tried to catch the straws in the wind, but by and large, we were all too overawed by the developments around us to make a constructive change or derive any vital advantage from the course of events. It is only now that we seem to be waking up to the implications of media convergence and the consolidation of different streams in the entertainment industry.

Fortunately, this feeling of realisation is being shared across the board, thereby preparing India for another phase of explosive growth. Media pundits are already talking of a 'second new wave', powered by the twin engines of technology and an enabling regulatory environment which will pitchfork India to the cutting edge of world competition. Accelerated digital connectivity, improved infrastructure for delivery platforms, immersive content media like IMAX theatres, the coming of age of FM and satellite radio and the emergence of new technologies like narrowcasting, microcasting and podcasting, are some of the possibilities which will help create the critical mass for the perceived launch and completely revolutionise the way we take to entertainment. For one, we will soon be distinguishing (in terms of time allocation) between in-home entertainment and out-of-home leisure fulfilment. For another, content variety will increase phenomenally (both in quantity and quality) and traditional market players will be forced to adapt or perish. Furthermore, regulatory bodies like TRAI (Telecom Regulatory Authority of India) will perforce have to create a liberal framework for the entertainment industry to flourish as also provide stronger protection mechanisms for copyrights and royalties.

All this, of course, will not happen overnight. In typical Indian conditions, changes do not occur gradually, but in fits and starts, affecting each sector in varying degrees, depending on its level of organisational maturity. As mentioned in the previous chapter, cinema, radio and, to an extent, television are considered the most matured segments of the entertainment industry, while music publishers, corporatised content producers and multi-system operators make for the maturing segments with the necessary aspiration

drive. The latter players are recognising the importance of raising the performance bar but, due to a variety of reasons (such as lack of expansion capital and the absence of professional human resources), have been able to achieve very little so far. The last and the least matured category is made up of clusters of local cable operators, theatre owners, music retailers and movie distributors who operate with short-term objectives and couldn't care less about planning ahead for sustained profits over extended periods. Nevertheless, they are important players in the value chain and contribute significantly towards the growth of the entertainment industry.

The role of each of these three clusters has to be evaluated in the context of the changing competitive environment, fuelled partially by the advent of alternative technologies. The nature and extent of their evolution is just as crucial. So also are the financial innovations, performance measurement mechanisms and process orientation measures being brought about which determine their strength, or vulnerability, whichever way you see it. From a filmmaker's point of view though, what matters ultimately is how he can selectively leverage the different initiatives to his advantage. Whether it is Aditya Chopra getting Abhishek Bachchan and Rani Mukherji, the con couple of *Bunty Aur Babli* (2005), to present news on television or Mahesh Manjrekar roping in a life insurance company to produce a teaser for his *Viruddh* (2005) or Prakash Jha launching an interactive website with information on kidnapping cases, film news and a blogger's space prior to the release of *Apaharan* (2005), Bollywood producers are increasingly aligning with alternative media to stand out in a crowd and ensure the biggest weekend rush to their films. Significantly, their efforts are yielding results.

According to a *Yes Bank* report on the Indian entertainment industry, the expansion of cable and satellite TV broadcasting in 2001 was the main decisive factor to have brought about a boost in the electronic marketing of Bollywood films. Between 2001 and 2005, the average marketing costs of the top 50 Hindi films rose from

Rs 5.2 million to almost double, Rs 10 million. Two-thirds of this amount was claimed by television while publicity through Internet and mobile telephony rose from 0 to 7 per cent of the budget during this period. The rest of the ad-spend was divided among outdoor hoardings and posters, press, radio, road shows and events. The point is, film producers now know that individual growth cannot be achieved in isolation, but has to be accompanied by taking other media players into the fold and it is with their support and active co-operation that the entire entertainment industry stands to gain. In the process, if marketing budgets balloon beyond 30 per cent of production costs and plain vanilla promotions of the dance-action-drama routine become history, so be it.

In all these projections we are missing one crucial point. Inter-dependence or integration of different sectors of the entertainment industry does not automatically guarantee benefits. In order to derive value, there have to be ways to drive value. And this is where margin pressures will come into play which, in effect, will draw attention to cutting costs and attaining sustainable efficiencies across the board. For film producers in particular, the key areas determining functional efficiencies are as follows:

- Organisation structure and its alignment to operational strategies.
- Streamlined processes, including mechanisms for measuring efficiency.
- Enhancing quality by inculcating best global practices.
- Strategic use of technology.
- Ensuring continuous improvements by consistent global benchmarking.

It is all very well to theorise and remind professionals about what they ought to do. But, as everybody knows, in a completely fractured and disorganised industrial environment, individual initiatives do not count for much. The ground rules should ideally be laid down

by a body like the Film Federation of India (FFI), or perhaps, the Association of Motion Pictures and Television Programme Producers (AMPTPP). But to expect either of these bodies to adopt a holistic approach towards operational effectiveness at the macro level will again be wishful thinking. In the circumstances, the only alternative is to look outwards and assimilate the experiences of pathfinders in other sectors. Learning from other regions and industries could greatly facilitate the desired performance turnaround as also ensure sustainability of benefits. After all, in a vast, developing country like India, more than what must be done, it is important to figure out what must *not* be done. And in this, there are valuable lessons that can be drawn from the IT, hospitality, aviation and pharmaceutical industries. They have all gone through the same teething problems the entertainment industry is experiencing at present, closed their ranks and, by projecting a united front, emerged stronger.

Once the opportunities (as well as roadblocks) are identified by the mainline players, the next step would be to improve the yield of an entertainment product—in this case, films. Very often, in our excitement to tap a fresh revenue stream, we overlook the potential of traditional sources which have sustained the industry for decades. A new discovery or technology upgrade does not always invalidate the old. For example, the opening up of possibilities on the Internet or mobile telephony does not nullify the potential of the good old box-office. Cinema (so long as it is recognised by that name) will have to address itself to the box-office. Likewise, in the case of television, subscriptions and airtime sales have been traditional sources of revenue. Tomorrow, if new opportunities like merchandising or exports open up, will the old marketing models be discarded? Generation of revenues from subscriptions and airtime sales will have to be pursued with the same vigour and efficiency as was done earlier. The new can only supplement the old and not be a replacement. The product will have to be made available to all interested consumers through every possible means of distribution. Only then will it be possible to maximise yield and optimise price levels.

Shifting Paradigms

The compulsions for such exploitation are guided by the increasingly perishable nature of entertainment as a commodity. It is here today, gone tomorrow. Whether it is cinema or television, radio or mobile telephony, Internet or live entertainment, if you have missed the moment, you have lost it for ever. In the old days, providers of such content could afford re-runs and repeat shows, but today they will be overtaken by competition. Nobody has any time (or space) for yesterday's leftovers, not even at night. Even retailers of music and DVDs/VCDs are not persisting with so-called 'popular hits'. For them, a week is a very long time to keep fresh stocks on the front racks. They have to replace them with still newer stocks, almost on a day-to-day basis. In a consumerist society, everybody lives by the moment.

Given this competitive scenario, what every entertainment producer needs is a steady stream of reliable data and information backup to plan his yield management initiatives. In the absence of a facilitating environment from the government, he has so far been going either by his gut feeling (which is actually not as unreliable as it is made out to be) or, by putting in place certain internal processes or systems to source market data. Most often, the information so derived is very sketchy and ridden with discrepancies. Any data gathering process should ideally provide for the following:

1. Demographic profiling of select markets, outlining consumer expectations and consumption patterns.

2. Communication blueprints (in terms of content, channels, etc.) and execution of publicity campaigns.

3. Distribution plans with emphasis on cost-effectiveness and yield maximisation.

4. Airtime inventory management and dynamic pricing.

5. Strategic product innovation.

6. Sales monitoring and course correction measures.

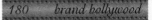

Film industries in the West have, for long, been benefiting from the facilities of active data gathering and warehousing systems which provide details of theatrical revenues, duly collated and analysed. More often than not, the system is front-ended by remote ticketing in order to enhance the reliability of data. Moreover, there are systems in place for audience tracking (both for films and television) to determine last mile consumption of entertainment. We too have such a mechanism in India, but meant largely for media buying on television. For films, no such system exists, barring the box-office reports by trade journals of dubious capabilities and repute.

It is high time Bollywood developed a reliable audience tracking mechanism, supported by adequate processes to help improve yield and minimise risks. Initially, such data collection may be undertaken on shared systems, as is done for, say, the tourism industry. Right from railway bookings to checking on the availability of hotel rooms and airline tickets, the Internet serves as a gateway to information for travel plans, accessible within minutes at the click of the mouse. For such an efficient and reliable data gathering from last mile points, a well-co-ordinated effort is required across the industry— at least till such time the necessary systems are put in place. This is not as difficult as it may sound, especially when industry players get to recognise the long-term commercial advantages from the initiative. Certain other key initiatives demanding attention of the film industry are as follows:

Alternative Revenue Streams

As the industry matures and entertainment consumption stabilises, Bollywood will have to identify alternative revenue opportunities. The exercise will begin from scripting and casting stages and extend to marketing and promotions with definite targets assigned for revenue generation. The focus areas are:

1. Taking cinema to newer geographic territories (e.g., selling Tamil films to the Japanese market).

2. In-film advertising and strategic use of commercial brands inside mainstream content.

3. Exploring merchandising options or supplementary programming, such as, publishing a book or making a documentary on how a certain film was made (e.g., *The Making of Lagaan*).

These are just a few examples suggestive of how key assets of a film can possibly be leveraged to raise higher revenues. In other words, producers will need to have the vision of enlarged revenue models with very clear action plans for their realisation.

Aggressive Marketing

Increased activity across genres and down the value chain will automatically spur demand for quality content. A combination of factors like emerging technologies, regulatory changes and growing awareness of a professional business approach will automatically ensure diversity of content at low initial investments and compelling value propositions. The challenge, however, lies in offering a choice of quality content by (*i*) subsidising consumer acquisition costs; and (*ii*) reduced premises equipment costs. Whoever is able to offer these twin facilities will emerge as the market leader. It will involve aggressive branding and distribution of content on the one hand, and imaginative re-engineering of the cost structure (through redistribution of risks and rewards) on the other. In time, production companies will have to develop low entry barriers and low cost business models and, according to their perceived viability, reset growth targets.

Newer Genres

Film production companies need to constantly define new genres according to the changing demographic profile of the market. The so-called tried and tested formulas of Hindi film-making are being constantly challenged and now the matinee idols and mega-stars are feeling the heat. Going by this trend, Bollywood cinema will soon cease to be personality-oriented and will increasingly veer around themes and treatment, as in the West. In a sense, this should suggest the maturing of Indian film-making, only that there is always the risk of a rash of 'me too' films trying to replicate the box-office record of earlier hits. Barring this herd mentality among film-makers,

audiences have every reason to look forward to more creativity and style on the Hindi screen, even if it might occasionally involve rekindling certain forgotten genres from the past.

Consumer Connect

While creativity in content creation will always be at a premium, the need to balance audience expectations with commercial realities cannot be overlooked. As has been mentioned earlier, producers will have to establish formal channels to strengthen consumer connect. It is not enough that systems are put in place to monitor or track consumer behaviour. The consumer would like to be heard and his is the voice that every producer of entertainment shall have to amplify in the development of content. The main reason for the failure of a large number of seemingly viable entertainment products (including films) is the huge gap in systemic research and feedback during the development stages. Consumer satisfaction surveys, profiling target segments and consumer support and complaint management processes in the last mile distribution will, to an extent, enable the transition to consumer focused businesses.

Talent Retention

In the face of stiff competition from sunrise industries, such as, BPO (business process outsourcing), software and aviation, the entertainment industry has to pull up its socks in attracting the best professional talent—both creative and managerial. Even more important is the prospect of retaining experienced talent. For this, it will be necessary to establish exciting and professional working environments, systems that measure and reward performance and, above all, clearly defined paths for career growth. Youngsters today are looking beyond monetary compensation while making career choices. The lure of glamour is also not enough. They are opting for value propositions that include growth potential, self-development and a lifestyle to match. The attractiveness of the industry will be further enhanced by setting up worldclass training institutes on the lines of the IITs and IIMs across the country.

Technology Adoption

Technology has a dual role to play in the entertainment business. Its adoption in the last mile distribution can drive demand and, in turn, growth of the industry. This has already been proved since the advent of interactive television, digital cinema, mobile devices, and so on. At another level, technology can serve as a process enabler for improving efficiencies and competitiveness. The potential, however, remains largely unexploited as core processes in film production, distribution and marketing are still conducted using legacy spreadsheets and primitive applications. Such lack of sophistication is not just a limiting factor in organisational effectiveness, but it also holds a significant risk from the perspective of business continuity. Unless producers increase their technology spend on filmmaking with qualitative long-term business justifications, the Indian entertainment industry will continue to lose out to the West.

Governance Standards

Entertainment businesses in India are typically family-run enterprises lacking in professional management, transparency, financial discipline and reporting. These factors adversely affect investor confidence, thereby placing the industry in a perpetual cash crunch spiral. With large corporate bodies and financial institutions evincing interest in aligning with entertainment producers, it is high time that the latter set their houses in order. The four pillars of good corporate governance are (*i*) transparent and efficient business practices, consistent with the law; (*ii*) active co-operation between the management and stakeholders in creation of wealth; (*iii*) timely and accurate disclosures on all material matters of the corporation; and (*iv*) accountability of the management to the company's stakeholders. Industry associations could possibly play a defining role in setting the standards for corporate governance. A committee to audit governance procedures adopted by members will further infuse efficiencies and bolster confidence among potential investors.

Industry Consolidation

No industry in India is as fragmented as the entertainment industry. Vast disparities between the few large players and multiple small players, all competing for the same market pie with a finite set of resources, have complicated matters further. As mentioned earlier, more than 90 per cent of Bollywood films are made by small independent producers, typically in the mid-budget range of Rs 20 to Rs 100 million, which are doomed for disaster. And yet, the contribution of this segment in terms of investments and the platform it provides for talent development cannot be underestimated. Moreover, who can stop anybody from making a film with whatever budgets he chooses? In the circumstances, what is necessary is a judicious utilisation of resources by initiating action at three different levels: (*i*) roping in established names with larger fan following to lower the *perceived* level of risk for investors; (*ii*) managing risk by spreading investments across multiple projects with varied themes and budgets; and (*iii*) equitable sharing of resources in terms of infrastructure and talent and, thereby, lowering project costs. The idea is very simply to build up scale efficiencies so that a consolidated growth path for the industry will emerge on its own.

▓ Regulatory Intervention

Inefficiencies across the value chain are the cause of many anomalies that not only lower profitability, but severely damage the credibility of the industry. Somehow, the bigger players have a way with tiding over adversities. But the smaller, independent content providers (including film-makers) have no such means, let alone the financial muscle or the resourcefulness to stay afloat for long. They are the ones who eventually pay the price for inefficiencies in the system. They are unable to upgrade their service and, as a result, the quality offered to the end consumer suffers. Ironically, they also end up contributing to the inefficiencies in the system. To the world at large though, the impression gaining ground is of the entertainment

industry in India being a high risk proposition where investments are unlikely to be ever safe. This translates into unwillingness on the part of financiers (particularly foreign) to stick their necks out, and the few who do, are charging unusually high rates of interest for the loans offered. Government financial institutions are no exception.

In the light of this analysis, industry participants will need to review their long-term development strategies and evaluate the desirability of inorganic growth. They will have to explore consolidation options in order to build up scale efficiencies. Costs on infrastructure and resources will only be going up, not down. From time to time, growth opportunities will keep emerging, but in a fragmented scenario— as different players keep cannibalising one another, nobody will be able to derive optimal benefits. This was precisely the problem being faced by the Indian telecom industry, till the government stepped in with a package of regulatory mechanisms. Much as the intervention has led to the creation of distorted structures within the industry, it could be a limited option worth considering for the short term, particularly by Bollywood. If anything, it would get the house in order. As the entertainment industry is at the threshold of a potentially steep growth curve, government regulators and film producers could perhaps sit together and lay out a clear agenda with practical initiatives for bringing about the desired level and quality of transformation.

Most modern economies in the West use selective and multi-dimensional regulatory or policy interventions to ensure growth and consumer choice. While the nature and extent of such interventions typically depend on the industry context and market dynamics, there are several common objectives which define the initiatives. In the case of Bollywood, as well as other sectors of the entertainment industry, the primary objectives for regulatory interventions would be as follows:

- protecting stakeholder and consumer interests
- ensuring adequacy of competition
- facilitating adoption of new technologies

- protecting investments
- ensuring business viability
- protecting intellectual property rights
- ensuring sustainable industry growth

Of these, fulfilling the very first objective—addressing the needs of stakeholders and consumers—will be more than half the battle won. The stakeholder universe of the entertainment industry includes content producers and owners, distributors, last mile access providers as well as related government bodies. Stakeholder interests originate from the extent and adequacy of competition in the entertainment value chain. The highest level of competition is among the mature players comprising film producers and distributors, theatre owners, music retailers, television broadcasters and unorganised providers of content. At the other extreme of this cluster are the corporate content producers and radio broadcasters, characterised by lower levels of competition and transparency. For them regulatory intervention becomes necessary because of revenue leakages from piracy and under-declaration, inequitable cost structures and existence of last mile monopolies. Besides, in a progressive democracy, there is always the question of affordability of entertainment products and the need to service lower income groups which need to be corrected.

Between these two levels of maturity among market players, there are the so-called 'growth engines' of the industry, such as, FM radio, DTH, IP-TV, mobile telephony, Internet, live entertainment organisers as well as digital movie distributors and exhibitors. This cluster represents the future of the Indian entertainment industry, not only for their increasing claims on the market share, but more significantly, because of their ability to function as the real agents of change. The government recognises their importance, but instead of creating a healthy operating environment for growth, treats them as milch cows by imposing a highly unjustifiable license and taxation regime. Many independent entrepreneurs with potential and having done well for themselves suddenly close shop, all because of their inability to deal with the unfairness of it all. Small wonder then that several

top-ranking film actors have, over the years, found it worthwhile to invest their earnings in ventures relating to real estate, pharmaceuticals, hotels and restaurants and even poultry farming, but not in the industry that gave them their millions in the first place. Only, of late, has there been a slight change of heart.

Given this skewed industrial scenario, it is ultimately the consumer's freedom of choice that gets compromised. This is already being experienced in the last mile of cable television services and, to an extent, in film and music distribution. The consumer has no right to subscribe to a content-quality-price combination of his preference. Neither does he have access to a grievance redressal mechanism in times of discrepancy between original product promise and functionality delivered. He cannot even demand prompt and effective service for the money he pays. All he can hope for is the free play of market forces which, in turn, will fuel competition and effectively raise the quality of product and services. The purpose of regulatory intervention is to encourage competition and not stifle growth. For example, in the case of broadcasting, the last mile segment where near monopolistic conditions exist in most parts of the country, government regulatory bodies could perhaps encourage the entry of alternative platform operators like DTH or IP-TV. Instilling insecurities in traditional players will automatically push the level of competition up, improve the quality of service and, most importantly, boost the momentum of growth in the industry.

As of now, most sectors of the entertainment industry are performing below optimum levels and, consequently, are unable to tap the opportunities opening up. The eventual realisation of their potential requires focused and co-ordinated action between stakeholders and regulators. For the past several years, television has been the prime mover for the industry. Till 2010 or so, it will continue to be the largest and fastest growing cluster, what with alternative platforms like DTH and IP-TV being introduced. The danger here is that other media like music, radio and even films might suddenly be starved of resources as funds get channelised to the more lucrative television sector. Here again, government intervention will become necessary

to ensure a balanced, all-round growth for the industry with special emphasis on the following:

- facilitating an investment-friendly environment for all sectors
- providing clarity in regulatory and policy announcements
- ensuring a level-playing field for healthy competition

In the absence of a focused approach, the whole exercise of opportunity exploitation becomes self-defeating and the industry could as well be struggling with a lopsided, disorganised and clueless growth path. The government regulator has to function not just as an agent for change, but it must also serve as a medium for bonding different segments of the industry and set a common sustainable growth path for all with appropriate incentives and penalties. In very specific terms, a regulatory charter, highlighting the following priorities across the sectors, would be in order:

- ensuring customer choice in all sectors
- improving customer service and redressal mechanisms
- rationalising licensing conditions
- improving last mile transparency
- ensuring non-discriminated access to content and platforms
- allowing operators the freedom to select a business model
- developing stringent anti-piracy penalties
- providing investment and operational incentives
- ensuring consistency and clarity in regulatory policies

These are high impact interventions demanding varying degrees of involvement from industry players, which may not be forthcoming during the initial stages. Bollywood is notoriously reticent towards any form of external interference, simply because of a collective mindset which perceives interventions as a threat to creative freedom. Moreover, it is known for its dogged refusal to look beyond next Friday. But once it is convinced about the long-term benefits of an

improved investment climate, a non-exploitative tax regime and the plugging of piracy leakages (without compromising creative freedom), there is no reason why film trade bodies should not fall in line one by one. Left to themselves, the trade associations are incapable of achieving anything of lasting value for the industry. They are far too involved with resolving petty partisan disputes to think long term for the larger good. And the FFI, which is supposed to provide a purpose and direction to the industry, has instead kept itself busy playing referee between the warring trade associations. With a well-meaning but authoritative regulatory body stepping in, all the associations representing diverse interests will come together and, perforce, have to raise their sights—to the extent of rejecting the regulator some day. This is a common experience of all booming industries the world over. Regulators have been rendered redundant the moment an industry finds its legs and begins to run.

Last Mile Environment

In the television sector, the issues are somewhat different. In fact, they are much more complex, even as there exists a semblance of order due to the fact that a majority of the players are already corporatised. This is one area where freelancers and fly-by-night operators can find no place. But there is no control on the tyranny of cable operators—the last mile segment, which raises questions of addressability. Since more that 75 per cent of Indian cable homes earn less than Rs 8,000 a month and the monthly subscription for around 100 channels has been pegged down to just Rs 150 on an average, mandatory implementation of addressability will instantly raise cable prices, leading to the shrinking of the subscriber base, which will, in turn, have a negative impact on advertising revenues. (In 2004–2005, the cost for maintaining 100 channels was estimated at Rs 350 per cable connection.) At the prevailing 30 per cent penetration, provision of CAS (conditional access system) with

secure STBs (set top boxes) will raise the monthly bill to beyond Rs 400 and an even worse spiral of reduced advertising revenues and inflated channel prices. A majority of entertainment channels will be beyond the reach of most consumers and for those who can afford the price hike, it would be a case of paying more to watch less.

These are aspects that Bollywood should be closely tracking as it gets heavily dependent upon the television medium, more so, with digitisation coming in. The point to be noted is that in no country has CAS been mandated to access pay content. Most countries consider migration to an addressable environment as part of a larger transition to a fully digital environment. In the U.S., the U.K., Australia and other advanced countries, industry players and regulators are committed to effect the transition as soon as a majority of cable homes are in a position to afford the migration. But in India, the decision to distribute television signals in an encrypted fashion and, therefore, force CAS on the consumer is purely a business decision of the cable operator. Now, from the point of view of television broadcasters and the government, denying a majority of consumers access to quality entertainment will considerably slow down the growth of the television industry. In the circumstances, the government (or a regulatory body) has no option but to evolve a framework for the classification of channels which will then enable television broadcasters (through consumer choice) to determine what is valued and what is not. The classification, as per international practice, would identify free-to-air channels, basic pay programming and a third category, i.e., premium tier programming. Accordingly, a price regulation can be enforced along with appropriate licensing of cable operators, thereby enhancing consumer choice and transparency in the last mile environment.

The last mile of entertainment service delivery is afflicted by yet another problem. As the most disorganised section of television broadcasting, it operates by its own set of rules, holding the consumer at ransom. For example, any dispute between cable operators and broadcasters often results in denial of consumer access to popular cricketing events without notice and nobody can do anything about it.

In a monopolistic situation, access has become an instrument of blackmail with no regard to consumer rights. No cable subscriber will independently take the fight to consumer courts without fear of risking life and limb. Here, it becomes necessary for the government to examine such abuse of power and devise implementable mechanisms to ensure appropriate service delivery and customer service. The mechanisms should clearly define the nature of service, level of standards and grievance redress for consumers.

Many media pundits believe that the only way of bringing about discipline in the last mile environment is to rationalise the licensing system. In the television space, no license is required for cable operators while unified licensing exists for DTH and IP-TV. Film or music distribution, exhibition and retailing do not require licenses. In radio, unviable licensing conditions (with hefty fee) are applicable. Such a disparate licensing regime has been a cause for concern. But in seeking to rationalise or, better still, harmonise the regime across platforms, there is always the danger of (*i*) jeopardising the commercial viability of one or the other sector; or (*ii*) robbing the medium of a level playing field. The other option is to introduce strict penal provisions, such as, fines for wrongful declarations, abusing consumer rights and non-compliance of service conditions. This will call for constant vigilance and monitoring of last mile operators, including surprise audits by authorised government bodies. By extension, the possibilities of multi-tiering the rating system for so-called 'adult content'—be it on films or for television—can also be expected.

There is one other way of weeding out trouble-makers in the last mile without inviting external intervention. And that can come by cross-media integration. It is a strategic tool employed by established business houses in order to gain a competitive edge in the market and, by default, eliminate the smaller players. In the entertainment industry, we have seen a television broadcaster acquiring strategic interests in movie exhibition and press; newspapers moving into radio, television, music sales and event management; a film processing lab taking on film production, distribution and running multiplexes—the idea is to offer integrated marketing solutions to a wide cross-section of consumer segments. These multi-media organisations do not abandon their core business in the course of such horizontal integration, but leverage their competence in it to strengthen their content and client relationships. There is also what is known as vertical integration, whereby a big fish eats the small fish to enhance its competitive positioning in the value chain and gain preferential or exclusive access to the distribution of content.

Both forms of integration take place all the time, often simultaneously and involving the same media organisation. The consolidation process sets off a kind of churning within the industry whereby the old jungle law of 'survival of the fittest' becomes applicable. The smaller players don't stand a chance in this scheme of things. If the example of the U.S. is taken, it will be found that the top 10 entertainment giants are integrated media players with interests in either multiple media or multiple segments of the value chain.

Walt Disney	Disney's interests span theme parks, hotels and consumer goods such as toys, and broadcasting, in addition to movies. The businesses are organised in the segments of media network, studio entertainment, theme parks and resorts and consumer products.
Viacom	Viacom is a leading global media company with interests in the creation, promotion and distribution of entertainment, news, sports, music and comedy. Viacom's well-known brands are CBS, MTV, Nickleodeon, VH1, BET, Paramount Pictures, Viacom Outdoor, Infinity, UPN, Spike TV, TV Land, Country Music Television, Comedy Central, Showtime, Blockbuster and Simon & Schuster.
Comcast	Comcast has interests spanning creation and distribution of content and is one of the leading players in cable television. Leading Comcast

(*continued*)

(continued)

	businesses include Comcast Cable, CN8.TV, E! Online, Comcast Spectator, Comcast Sports, Philadelphia Flyers, 76ers, Golf Channel and Outdoor Life Network.
Newscorp	Newscorp is an integrated media company with interests in publishing, film and television production, broadcasting and distribution, network stations and radio.
Clear Channel	Diversified media businesses spanning television, radio, outdoor leisure and recreation.
NBC	The oldest network in the U.S. owned by General Electronics. Its assets include NBC, CNBC, MSNBC, Bravo Cable Network and Telemundo. NBC has also invested in History Channel, Value Vision and Praxis Communication Corporation.
AOL/Time Turner	Integrated media and communication company with interests in the creation and distribution of content. The group businesses include AOL, Time Warner Cable, Time, HBO and CNN.
Cox Comm	Cox is an integrated distribution play offering voice, data, broadcasting and pay-per-use services.
Echostar	Integrated satellite-based distribution player. Owns Dish TV.

Thus, the lesson for India is simple: If you want to be big in the entertainment business, you cannot afford to be a stand-alone company for long. At some stage, you will have to acquire, align, diversify and consolidate. The process could lead to monopolies, with all the attendant evils of anti-competitive behaviour and discriminatory practices. There is also a possibility of the entertainment company collapsing under its own weight if it is unable to generate custom. After all, more than any other perishable commodity, entertainment products are habit forming and count heavily on

customer loyalty. The entry of a mega multi-media player with deep pockets in an entertainment space does not automatically guarantee a loyalty shift. But it does ensure the following benefits to the industry:

1. infusion of new capital and heightened optimism for accelerated growth;

2. requisite technology for enhanced programme/content quality; and

3. significant investments for transition to the digital last mile.

Moreover, it is possible to evolve safeguards against abuse of the advantages arising out of integrated media businesses. Many countries have formulated regulations on cross media holdings and mandatory access obligations so as to check the possibilities of any such abuse. We may similarly insist upon obligations like 'Must Carry' and 'Must Provide' through a regulatory body. In fact, a section of the industry is already talking about upgrading the TRAI (Telecom Regulatory Authority of India) to that of a National Convergence Regulator. In this role, it will enjoy the regulatory overview of all businesses dealing with the carriage of voice or data, including information, news and entertainment over cable, fibre, copper, wireless and radio. So long as it shares the passion of the industry and enables it to evolve and prosper in a transient economy, there can be no issue. But problems would arise the moment it imposes restrictive regulations that amount to stifling growth. On that contentious issue, it is always better to revert to market forces as the final arbiter.

ten

Back to the Future

In the new emerging global entertainment order, it is 'advantage India' at present. Whichever way you see it, Indian cinema and, more specifically, Bollywood films stand the best chance in challenging Hollywood's hegemony in the movie making world. In terms of numbers, mass appeal, technical finesse and talent pool, we are already streets ahead of the Chinese, the only other important global player. New territories like Greece, South Korea and Morocco are opening up to Mumbai's '*masala* mix' of songs and dances. At overseas film festivals, people are no longer pretending to be unaware of Bollywood and raising foolish questions like 'Amitabh Bachchan, Who?' or 'Am I supposed to know Aishwarya Rai?' Foreign film-makers, artistes and technicians are all coming to shoot in India. Besides, right from the Italians to the Australians to the South Africans, Uzbeks and the sheikhs of the Middle East, everybody is anxious to invite Bollywood film-makers and stars to work in their midst. These are other than the traditional locations in the Swiss Alps and the beaches of Seychelles and Mauritius, where Indian film crews are almost permanently stationed. Also, with the frequent exchange of artistes and technicians, we are headed to a time when Batman might open his mask to reveal the face of a grinning Bollywood actor!

These are indicators which augur well for the future. But then, on second thoughts, what's so new about all this? If the Greeks are discovering Shahrukh Khan now and Rakesh Roshan feels compelled to dub his films in Spanish, there was similar excitement in 1947

when V. Shantaram broke into the U.S. market by screening *Shakuntala* in a New York theatre. Two years later, K.A. Abbas's *Dharti Ke Lal* (1949) debuted in Russia, preparing the ground for Raj Kapoor and *Awara* in 1954. The same year Bimal Roy's *Do Bigha Zamin* (1954) won the top awards at Cannes and Karlovy Vary. Satyajit Ray was to follow later. Today, if Shahrukh Khan and Amitabh Bachchan are regarded as brand ambassadors for Bollywood, there were several such high profile (if not more accomplished) personages to represent Indian cinema in the past. Likewise, this is not the first time Hindi films are finding mention in the Oscar nominations or at the many overseas film festivals like Venice, Berlin and Cannes. In the same manner, our film-makers have been shooting abroad, in places like Tokyo and Paris in the past, just as they are doing in Switzerland and elsewhere now. In the past, actors ranging from I.S. Johar to Victor Banerji, Kabir Bedi and Amrish Puri have worked in Hollywood films. There was also a time when the trio of Om Puri, Shabana Azmi and Naseeruddin Shah made for the Asian face of Hollywood cinema. Today, it is the turn of Salman Khan and Aishwarya Rai.

Thus, the more things change, the more they appear to be the same. We continue to be doing what has already been done in the past, only that the competition among film-making nations (China included) was not as intense then. Besides, it is not as though we are doing anything differently or more imaginatively than what our predecessors did. In our eagerness to break away from the beaten track and explore new genres in film-making, we remain stuck in a rut, to the extent of persisting with remakes of old classics like *Sahib Bibi Aur Ghulam* and *Parineeta*. All that we have achieved in the process is packaging old wine in new bottles. In the past, everybody was anxious to break the barrier between mainstream and parallel cinema. Today, the same anxiety prevails, only that they have given it a new name—crossover cinema. Co-productions with foreign film companies, which began during the thirties, peaked during the seventies and eighties and are still continuing in bits and spurts. Furthermore, we tend to make a song and dance of the production houses run by people like Yash Chopra, Subhash Ghai, Karan Johar and Ram Gopal Varma.

In what way are they different from the studio system nurtured by the likes of V. Shantaram, Sasadhar Mukherji, Dev Anand and Raj Kapoor? Today, of course, the explanation given for this revival is 'value chain integration'.

Thus, in being stuck to the past, Bollywood has failed to acquire the stature where a Hindi film-maker might be able to stand up and boldly claim to have gone global with his film. This is what separates us from the big boys. Nobody among us has yet thought of making a biographical on, say, Marilyn Monroe or Nelson Mandela. (Think about it: What is wrong in casting a foreign actor in the title role of a Bollywood film?) They are familiar names among Indians. We had to wait for Richard Attenborough to be in our midst and make *Gandhi* (1980) and, thereafter, we followed suit with a rash of biographical films on freedom fighters ranging from Bhagat Singh to Subhas Chandra Bose and Chandrashekhar Azad. At all other times, we are shamelessly copying what Hollywood does, whether it is *Basic Instinct* (1992) or *Reservoir Dogs* (1992), *Godfather* (1972) or *Love Story* (1970). Even on music and choreography, not to mention the gimmicks that pass for special effects, we always look westwards for inspiration. Given half a chance, Bollywood film-makers would get a white-skinned dancer to do an item number for them, but not consider doing a film with actors of different nationalities (as Peter Brooks did for *Mahabharata* [1989]). Nothing prevents anybody from taking these initiatives. Apart from mythology, we do not have the mindset to produce a decent adventure film, a social drama or a fantasy of the *Harry Potter* kind. These are themes holding universal appeal that instantly click with an international audience. Given our rich literary heritage, several such exciting themes and story ideas can be exploited from time to time. But we are afraid of even considering them because of a mental block inherited from the past. We wait for somebody else to take the first plunge and then, perhaps, decide whether to follow. The day we get over this reticence, is the day we can claim to have become truly global.

Oddly enough, Bollywood's fortunes have traditionally depended upon a clutch of barely five or six big producers who tend to be the cornerstones of the Hindi film industry from time to time. There are now barely half-a-dozen such production houses calling the shots by virtue of a formidable track record and capabilities built over the years. Their experience enables them to operate with greater efficiency compared to the rest of the industry and manage practically all the elements of the value chain—film-making, finance, distribution, exhibition, music sales and satellite broadcasting. Many of them have turned into corporate bodies, though in a very limited manner. More often than not, there is no clear delineation between creative and management functions as the promoter/CEO doubles up as the chief creative person, getting involved in every stage, from script selection to casting to location hunting, filming, post-production, sales, and so on. The rest of the staff members, including senior executives, are left to function as operational managers. Consequently, if a comparison is made on the level of efficiency between Bollywood and Hollywood on any of the following eight counts, we will be found tragically wanting:

- writing and development of scripts
- pre-production—finalising the crew, casting, location selection, etc.
- above-the-line cost control
- below-the-line cost control
- risk reward sharing and mitigation
- contracts and documentation
- product marketing
- merchandising

Based on established film-making practices of the West, a proper corporatised approach to the business would imply a mix bag of initiatives and actions on the part of the CEO (in our case, the producer-director) of the production house:

- Intelligent selection of scripts, factoring in audience preferences and market trends.

- Projection of feasibility analysis of target audience preferences, box-office results, talent popularity and story viability in domestic and international markets.

- Active participation and consent of each activity head at the green-lighting stage.

- Investing in equipment, technology and management information systems so as to bring down costs and build in flexibility in shooting schedules.

- Control over production timelines, budgets and quality with periodic monitoring.

- Outsourcing non-critical functions, so as to concentrate more effectively on the core aspects of film-making.

- Introducing a profit sharing system among partners, thereby reducing initial risk on upfront payments.

Clearly, it is time we start benchmarking with the best global practices. Corporatisation, of course, enables this. But unlike other industries where a system of quality control can be enforced, cinema does not allow for certification of standards. (In Bollywood parlance though, some form of arbitrary classification of films is done on the lines of High Grade, Medium Grade and Low Grade.) Nevertheless, in a corporate environment, it is not very difficult to enforce the practices of scalability, technology upgradation and ethical conduct to film-making. Only then will it be possible to draw and retain the best and the brightest professionals in the industry as well as attract a high level of foreign investment. Without transparency (especially in financial dealings) and fairness (in day-to-day operations), the confidence of stakeholders (including employees) is bound to be disturbed, and that will reflect in the quality of the product projected on screen.

Corporatisation holds other blessings as well:

- Instilling a culture of self-restraint and discipline in the film-making process.

- Placing high emphasis on matters relating to planning and documentation.

- Enforcing cost control measures at every stage of production.

- Better sharing of common resources.

- Ensuring a high degree of accountability from every member of the production unit.

- Integration and rightsizing of all functions down the value chain.

- Consolidation among fragmented players in the industry.

- Developing an institutional memory of the best practices.

On account of these reasons, a corporate producer stands a far better chance at obtaining institutional finance than a private film-maker. Ever since film-making was recognised as an industrial activity, banks and credit institutions have been fairly liberal with loans on easy terms, but mainly to corporate film-makers. Between 2001 and 2004, almost 100 films had availed of institutional funding to the tune of Rs 7 billion. It is believed that this figure will grow considerably in the future if (*i*) on the demand side, Bollywood creates an environment conducive to institutional funding; and (*ii*) on the supply side, more financiers enter the fray, thereby spreading the risk for a single financier and deepen the market.

Portfolio Management

These initiatives towards corporatised film-making have, significantly enough, neither been inspired by Hollywood nor motivated by some radical thinking management guru. The seeds of a disciplined and organised approach were already sown in southern India where the average time frame for completing a big-budget film is between 4 and 9 months as against the 15 to 18 months that Bollywood takes for almost the same kind of production. In fact, India's first corporate film production house to be listed in the stock exchange, G.V. Films Ltd., was set up by film-maker Mani Ratnam's elder brother, late G. Venkateshwar in Chennai during the eighties.

At that time it had been established that Tamil cinema was notching a consistently far higher degree of efficiency and professionalism than Bollywood, primarily because of three reasons:

- Appropriate importance given to script development and pre-production.

- Lead actors working on a limited number (usually one or two) of films at a time.

- Scale of operations allowing studios (*i*) a greater degree of integration and sharing of common resources; and (*ii*) the flexibility to amortise as well as spread costs and risks over a larger portfolio.

Notwithstanding Bollywood's limited understanding of modern corporate dynamics, producers like Ram Gopal Varma and Yash Chopra have successfully taken these ideas forward to strike economies of scale with multiple productions launched almost simultaneously. Rather than produce the costliest film of the year, they have been utilising the same available resources to make a portfolio of cost-effective films in a year. Essentially, they are playing it safe by blending films of different genres and budget segments aimed at different markets and different audiences. In times to come, this will be the most pragmatic course open to the bigger producers who have the funds and are particular about dissipating their risk profile. Moreover, it has been estimated that these so-called 'portfolio producers' will be able to reduce their costs by 10 to 12 per cent should they (*i*) own the studio infrastructure and equipment; (*ii*) sign long-term contracts with artistes and technicians; and (*iii*) enter into multiple contracts with distributors and exhibitors.

Effectively, what we are looking at is a step forward from the studio system of yore. On a simple calculation, a 10 per cent reduction in costs coupled with a 15 per cent increase in revenue can more than double the industry's profits in the medium term. This is exactly the objective Bollywood producers should be setting for themselves, individually and collectively, for starters.

But how do these benefits come about? Typically, on the outflow side of a film portfolio, the heads of expenditure are pre-production (2 per cent of the budget), artistes' costs (30 per cent), post-production (7 per cent), equipment hire (4 per cent), production (35 per cent) and, finally, distribution including print and publicity (22 per cent) costs. Cost mitigation through planned strategies can easily shave 10 per cent on artiste's costs (not on the fee), reducing it to 27 per cent of the overall filming budget. Distribution costs can be conveniently cut by 14 per cent on an average, reducing it to 19 per cent. These are usually the two key areas that tend to be over-budgeted. The third head involving high wastage levels is production. This can be reduced to 30 per cent (from 35 per cent), while the budget for pre-production may be doubled to 4 per cent. Possible savings on post-production and equipment could be 2 per cent and 1 per cent, respectively. In all, savings of at least 10 per cent of the budget can be achieved in an average Bollywood production by adopting these obvious cost-cutting devices.

Now, let us turn to the inflow side, where revenue streams are usually identified as domestic theatrical (normally 65 per cent), overseas theatrical (11 per cent), satellite rights (14 per cent), music (6 per cent) and others (4 per cent). It has been estimated that by plugging leakages (due to piracy and under-declaration of receipts), domestic theatrical receipts can easily be raised by 9 to 14 per cent. Even if no change is made in the figures of all other sources, the risk-reward ratio works out to 25 per cent-plus. With economies of scale coming into play, returns can go up to 40 per cent, thus lowering the risk perception on the project and collectively leading to a complete turnaround of the film company and, by extension, of the industry as a whole.

But then, how many of our film-makers will willfully adopt the portfolio approach? Barring a few self-righteous sorts, who are compelled by conscience or vigilant auditors (for the purposes of filing tax returns), Bollywood producers generally abhor all forms of accounting—and accountability. They are more comfortable with verbal assurances and act on hunches rather than be caught dealing with documents.

How else will you explain producers gifting away houses and cars to their actors and choreographers? Even today, playback singers keep much of their money, not in banks, but in water tanks, wrapped in polythene bags. Where does the money come from? A majority of Bollywood film-makers cannot claim a single hit to their names and, yet, they live in huge mansions, collect cars for a hobby, throw lavish parties, maintain mistresses in five-star suites, holiday abroad with their families and still have enough money to launch another potential dud.

It is for all these reasons that Bollywood film folk are viewed with suspicion. Never has there been a culture of financial discipline in the Hindi film industry. Commercial lending agencies have constantly shied away from being part of their dubious enterprises, leaving (*i*) high net worth individuals, and (*ii*) distributors and music companies to step in and pay advances at usurious rates of interest. The odd part though is that with all the attendant risks, private funding has not been in short supply, even during lean periods. For instance, in 2002—the *annus horribilis* for Bollywood—fresh capital kept pouring in and, wonder of wonders, remained largely unspent. Clearly, the industry was able to generate sufficient returns, despite the high financing costs. It also implies that in the absence of proper accounting procedures and reliable costing data, the costs of production may have been grossly overstated. Obviously, the bottom-line for the industry has to be much healthier than what is usually projected to be.

This probably explains why some banks and financial institutions had decided to stick their necks out the moment the government granted recognition to the film industry in 2000. To an extent, the organised funding reduced average financing costs. But what usually gets overlooked is that when compared to the lending rates in other sectors, institutional finance for film projects is significantly higher. Additionally, stipulations like completion bonds, insurance and well-defined contracts have come into play. The bank typically finances up to 50 per cent of a project and retains the negative rights as collateral. The producer puts in the rest of the money from his own

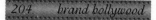

sources. The bank also insists on a completion guarantee from the producer and insurance against possible delays. Risk taking is thus shared equitably.

With the portfolio approach being thus forced on (though still in a limited manner) film-makers by banks and others, rating agencies now feel encouraged to undertake independent evaluation of projects and, in effect, facilitate the availability of specialised guarantee funds to mitigate the risks of the financial institution. Such so-called 'credit enhancers' are expected to bring about a revolutionary impact on the financing structure of the Bollywood industry. Banks and government lending institutions should soon be taking a larger share of the risk, say, up to 70 per cent of the project budget. It is also conceivable that the interest rates for such finance could drop sharply because the risk of the lender is reduced considerably.

A step beyond this (and well within the realm of possibility) will be the time when film financing will not be project-specific, but a working capital loan extended to a corporate entity owning the entire value chain. In this futuristic scenario, the loan will be securitised against exhibition receivables—not only from theatres, but also through the last mile integration of television, music, home video, mobile telephony and Internet channels. For the lending institution, the risk capital will be spread across a portfolio of projects with the production company as an equal partner in the venture. (A beginning has already been made in this direction as corporate houses are backing select producers with a corpus of funds meant to finance a basket of films. Sahara did this with Ram Gopal Varma in 2003.) The dream of every film-maker will, however, be to earn a reputation where his name, rather than the films he intends to make, will attract an ensemble of financiers on competitive terms.

The outcome of these possibilities is not hard to imagine. For one, the Hindi film industry will perforce have turned more transparent and disciplined in all matters concerning finance. For another, funds will be forthcoming from legitimate sources and at cheaper rates. Third, in this increasingly surcharged professional environment, only films motivated by business sense rather than passion will get beyond the approval stage. Fourth, as a consequence of the shrinking of unorganised finance, the quantum of films produced annually will drop sharply. And finally, the average cost of production per film is bound to increase with larger allocations made on script development, pre-production, visual effects and marketing. In time, these benefits will percolate down to films made in regional languages across India.

 Global Powerhouse

While these developments will doubtless place the Indian film industry on a very firm footing, a far bigger challenge lies elsewhere, in the exploitation of the international market. At present, there are three key market territories where Bollywood cinema has found a degree of acceptance:

- Indian diaspora, mainly in the U.S., the U.K., South Africa, Canada and the Middle East. The biggest concentration of settlers of Indian extraction in the world is in Myanmar (almost twice that of the U.S.), but they remain largely untouched by Bollywood owing to political and diplomatic restrictions.

- Neighbouring countries where Hindi is understood, if not spoken, that is, Pakistan, Nepal, Bangladesh, Sri Lanka and Malaysia. The success of Bollywood cinema in these markets is, however, driven not by content but by the popularity of lead performers.

- Non-traditional/new markets like Greece and the CIS (Commonwealth of Independent States) countries where Hindi films were extremely popular till around the early seventies. Bollywood cinema is now revisiting these countries, but with subtitled or dubbed content.

For India to emerge as a global powerhouse and earn sustainable export revenues, it is imperative to look beyond these markets with a wider portfolio of content, not necessarily limited to a few block-busters. Sadly, the tendency has so far been to promote only those films which are already hits at home and ignore the rest. Added to this is the fact that most foreign distributors of Indian films have very limited understanding of the potential of Bollywood cinema. Earlier, they were fixated on Satyajit Ray and Mrinal Sen. Today they have shifted their attention to the likes of Buddhadev Dasgupta and Adoor Gopalakrishnan. Not only are their films easy to market, but they also come at a price far cheaper than a multi-starrer by, say, Abbas-Mustan or Boney Kapoor. There is no way they will commit any investments for a mainstream Bollywood potboiler in these circumstances.

Producers like Yash Chopra and Karan Johar understood very early how they were handicapped in dealing with the prejudices of foreign distributors and, for better or worse, started distributing their films on their own steam. They need to now go one step further and forge independent tie-ups with global distribution majors so that their films secure a mainstream release, rather than be confined to sub-standard, India-centric theatres abroad. For all others, things have become much easier with marketing agents now mediating to forge alliances with leading distributors worldwide. This has been the practice in Hollywood for long. Independent producers there have neither the contacts nor the resources to build relationships with distributors across countries. Marketing agents form the critical bridge between the producer and the distributor. Agents familiar with Bollywood cinema and with also an understanding of different markets and their revenue streams may be hard to come by at present. But in time, they will be holding the key to the success of Hindi films across the globe.

This is, however, not to undermine the importance of good quality *entertaining* cinema. We are continually upping our standards, with better production values, improved subtitling and dubbing and engrossing content. Now, more importantly, it will be the ability to handle a large canvas and narrate a story, keeping in mind an international audience that shall place Bollywood at the cutting edge of

competition. This has been the recipe for success for all the India-centric films made by Hollywood biggies, right from David Lean (*Passage to India* [1984]) to Richard Attenborough (*Gandhi* [1980]) and Ronald Joffe (*City of Joy* [1992]). Later, Mira Nair and Shekhar Kapur were to apply the same formula to create a niche for themselves in Hollywood.

The good thing about Hollywood, if one were to notice, is that it has never been a closed house. From Fred Zinnemann and Milos Forman to Billy Wilder, Roman Polanski and Elia Kazan, its greatest directors have all been from the non-English speaking world. Apart from benefiting from this cross-fertilisation of talent, Hollywood has proved time and again that more than language and geographies, it is the ability to tell a story in an interesting manner that eventually finds appreciative audiences. Where you are located is immaterial; so long as you have it in you to keep the audience engaged, you could well be working from Iceland and churning out hits with a Hollywood studio tag. The very fact that Bollywood film-makers, actors, music composers and, of late, choreographers are increasingly finding work abroad proves that cinema knows no geographical boundaries.

Furthermore, the importance of inviting global majors to align with us through co-production and other collaborative deals has to be emphasised. Not many Indians know that the landmark film from Hong Kong, *Crouching Tiger, Hidden Dragon* (2000) (which reportedly grossed U.S.$ 140 million worldwide) was actually produced by a Hollywood consortium. Warner Bros, similarly, have huge interests in the film industry in the Philippines. The Miramax-produced Chinese film, *Hero* opened to a massive U.S.$ 18 million collection in August 2004, surpassing the combined receipts of all other Hollywood films during the week of its opening. It went on to gross well over U.S.$ 100 million in box-office receipts worldwide.

Elsewhere in Asia, countries like South Korea and Japan, which had nothing to claim by way of exports till 1997, are now riding at the crest of an unprecedented boom with business crossing the 100 million mark annually in the U.S. alone—thanks entirely to

collaborations with Hollywood studios. In comparison to all these countries, India figures nowhere, despite being in an eminently privileged position. Apart from production capacity and know-how, we are among the few countries which have successfully resisted the invasion of Hollywood cinema. Hollywood films command barely 4 per cent of the market share in India, the lowest it has dipped anywhere in the world. So, while other countries with vibrant film industries like France, the U.K. and China have buckled under the onslaught of Hollywood films, we have steadfastly maintained our production record. And this, without having to resort to state inter-vention or control mechanisms (like limiting the exhibition of foreign films or other such protectionist measures) which other countries have adopted.

Consequently, no matter what other nations are up to, India should ideally be calling the shots and be where Hollywood is today. We should be the ones attracting global talent as well as finance for multinational collaborations. There is no reason why, say, *The Mahabharata* cannot be recreated on the same scale and grandeur as *Troy* (2004) was, in collaboration with three or four international production houses. Similarly, the character of the monkey king, Hanuman, lends itself to the making of a top class blockbuster with the same finesse and hi-jinks as a *Superman* (1988). There are several such characters in Indian mythology, literature and history which make for supremely successful collaborative ventures. The cost-advantage that India affords, coupled with the absence of restrictions on FDIs (foreign direct investments), should only be allowing greater flexibility in scaling up budgets and technical capabilities necessary for producing movies on a global scale.

Finally, there is the vastly unexplored area of remakes of successful Indian films. We are constantly adapting Tamil to Hindi, Bengali to Hindi, English to Hindi, but how many Hindi films have been made for an international audience in English? For some odd reason, we seem content if a dubbed version finds a buyer abroad. At the most, a Bollywood film-maker might shoot two versions of the same film—one for the domestic market and the other for a so-called

'international audience'. Invariably, the latter is just an abridged version of the Hindi (derived out of eliminating the songs), and the furthest it can go is to an overseas film festival. Everywhere else, re-making films in English on a completely different setting and with a new cast and crew is a highly successful and well-established business practice. For instance, *The Ring* (1998) was a Hollywood remake of a fabulously popular Japanese horror film, *Ringu* and had grossed around U.S.\$ 130 million globally. Vidhu Vinod Chopra entered into one such deal with *Munnabhai MBBS* in 2005. But as they say, 'one swallow does not make a summer'.

Let us face it—we are all conscious of our capabilities as a film-making nation and what it takes to be a global super power at par with Hollywood; but we lack the will to go that extra mile in translating our potential into practice. We seek quick-fix solutions, mainly to tide over immediate problems. This short-sightedness stems from our inbuilt insecurities which make us look at one another as competitors, if not rivals. Even Hollywood is considered a rival. The practice of partnering progress in a spirit of collaboration and fruitful co-existence is still alien to us. Along with this, the foresight required to create an environment conducive to foreign investments has been sorely lacking. All that an investor looks for before committing funds for any venture is that his money should be safe. Multiplying the money and reaping profits come later. So long as a film-maker is transparent in his dealings and demonstrates a degree of financial rectitude, attracting foreign investments for projects of a global scale can never be an issue. After all, financial probity is the key to creating investor confidence.

Road Map Ahead

A comparison of the stages of film production in India (Bollywood in particular) with that of Hollywood will reveal that we tend to overlook the most basic process of production—the development of an idea. During this stage, typically, the story is developed from a nebulous concept to a script in hard copy with a provisional screenplay. In Hollywood, the commercial viability of this script/screenplay is evaluated carefully by way of market segmentation, audience research and box-office projections, using advanced forecasting models. Obtaining filming rights, signing of the cast and crew and the raising of capital constitute part of the development process. On an average, all this takes between three and four years in Hollywood and only 20 per cent of the stories processed at this stage move on to the next stage, that is, pre-production. This is despite Hollywood boasting of an integrated studio system, which oversees all aspects of the value chain. In Bollywood we should be taking even longer at the development stage, given all our handicaps, including the fragmented and unorganised nature of the industry. But then, our anxiety is always to transfer the risk to the next link in the value chain rather than manage the overall risk efficiently. Impatience and the lack of necessary budgets for script development and market research manifest themselves in the relative non-profitability of Bollywood cinema, despite its growing revenues every year.

Significantly, it is at the production stage that Bollywood spends more time than Hollywood. The reasons are obvious: cost overruns, bad planning and interruptions in the flow of funds (particularly for middle and low-budget films). In the post-production stage, again we spend lesser time than our U.S. counterparts because of (*i*) funds invariably getting exhausted due to overshooting the budget; and (*ii*) haste in releasing the film in order to recover investments faster. Another crucial difference between Hollywood and Bollywood is that while the former attaches considerable attention and funds to the promotion of its films, we leave it to the distributors to carry the entire burden of marketing on their shoulders. Inevitably, this leads to (*i*) the distributor suffering from a working capital crunch due to the failure of one film and the inability to generate funds for marketing the next one; and (*ii*) each distributor using his own discretion in promoting a film and, in effect, conveying a message which could be at odds with what the producer or director intends to. Eventually,

a good film could well fall flat at the box-office for no fault of the film-maker and his crew.

These are serious concerns for the industry, especially when it becomes apparent how we are losing out on opportunities from the emerging entertainment scenario worldwide. The shape of things to come will, to a large extent, be determined by the younger generation of directors, producers and distributors, and their understanding of the implications of convergence of film-making technology with the rest of the media, including Internet. Already digital content has become an integral part of well-known Hollywood blockbusters like *The Matrix* (1999), *Twister* (1996) and *Jurassic Park* (1993). India could not be part of this revolution despite its talent pool of world class software professionals. In every other way, the nation stood out as a major outsourcing destination by virtue of its ability to offer end-to-end services of the desired quality to discerning international customers. But in film-making, the highest achievement we can claim is of offering cost-effective services limited to animation and special effects. No Indian studio has yet been able to integrate all the segments of the value chain and offer end-to-end services for any major global film producer.

But then, nothing is lost. However interested we might have been in taking up back-end jobs for overseas producers, we just did not have the necessary studio infrastructure to back our capabilities. The most modern studio in India till about 2002–2003 was located near Hyderabad—the Ramoji Rao Film City—and all it could boast of was hiring out equipment, crew, sets and post-production facilities to Hollywood productions, such as, the Oscar-winning *Gladiator* (2000). It is only recently that a few medium-sized visual effects studios have come up in other parts of India with infrastructure matching international standards. Most importantly, these establishments are all working well below their true capacities and at a relatively low end of the value chain. It is, therefore, clear that the potential which was absent earlier, exists now. The moment this fact catches the attention of the Hollywood biggies and one or two studios in Mumbai prove that they are able to deliver, the level of

dependence on the Indian film industry will rise automatically. Till then, we will have to continue devising appropriate measures in terms of quality control and building sets of skills necessary to move up the value curve.

Another factor in our favour is that as a major outsourcing destination, India has earned the confidence of more than 50 per cent of the Fortune 500 companies. India handles over U.S.$ 12 billion of back-end business operations annually and has been maintaining a steady growth of 30 per cent on an average. Already, this has had a ripple effect across the board and our film industry is benefiting from it. Also, strangely enough, the concentration of back-end post-production work in films has a way of shifting from one country to another according to the changing political climate, quality of output and relative cost-advantages, from time to time. For many years, the U.S. outsourced much of its post-production work to the British film industry. Then Australia moved in to take the place of the U.K. Right now, it continues to be the back-end hub for a majority of outsourced Hollywood films. Very soon, it could well be India's turn—purely on the strength of its 2.5 million strong skilled workforce and, above all, the cost-advantage it presents. Between the U.S. and India, the cost differential on film production and processing is as high as 1,000 per cent!

Even on grounds of topography, the nation has so much to offer. The variety of backdrops and colour we can boast of—ranging from the snow-capped mountain ranges of the north to the warm coastal waters and beaches of the south, the large tracts of dense forests in the north-east to the vast desert expanses in the west. Nowhere on earth does nature reside in its magnificent splendour as in India. And yet, foreign film units are heading towards Australia, South Africa, Canada and even Spain for the very same backdrops we have here. *The Matrix* (1999) was filmed in Australia, *Shanghai Knights* (2003) was shot in the Czech Republic, *Anaconda* (1997) was set in Indonesia, *Kill Bill* (2003) in China, *The Entrapment* (1999) in Malaysia. After *Gandhi* (1980), no major foreign film has been shot on Indian soil, all because of one unfortunate fact—the perception producers

abroad hold about India. The crowds, unhygienic hotels, logistical problems and, above all, bureaucratic red-tapism have together conspired in projecting a negative image of India over the years. It is only now that the government has realised how damaging this perception has been and, in line with countries like South Africa and New Zealand, is adopting a 'single window system' for the clearance of all foreign shoots in India. Such a facilitative regulatory environment, coupled with a focused promotion drive, will go a long way in making India a major international shooting destination.

In other areas also, the government can play a proactive role as an enabler and facilitator for its film industry. But it will not. Bollywood's wish-list may keep on extending, but the government will not offer tax incentives in any form to any sector of the industry, let alone amortise production costs of big budget ventures (as in other countries), reduce customs duty on imports of studio and other equipment or even allot land for developing additional infrastructural facilities and training institutions. Bollywood will have to resort to its own devices if it has to effect the transformational modifications necessary for launching on the path of sustained growth. As has repeatedly been explained earlier, these would involve several strategic and structural alterations, implementation of new technologies, superior understanding of the audience pulse and better organisational efficiency. Only then will Bollywood, in particular, and the entertainment industry, in general, realise its true potential.

Ultimately, it all boils down to a question of choices. In this time and age, nobody can pretend to remain oblivious to the revolutionary changes brought about by the new entertainment order. But still, you can always dig your head into the sand and refuse to take cognisance of the changes around you, come what may. At the most, you might opt for the convenience of allowing yourself to drift with the tide and take each day as it comes. This is actually what we have been doing for so long. The other option is to adapt and imbibe business processes that will force changes to your advantage. This way, you will be taking a proactive course and will be part of the change. By exploiting the right technologies and adopting

Index

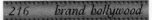

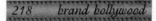

Derek Bose is a senior journalist and film jurist. He is also the group editor with a leading publishing house in Mumbai, which publishes lifestyle magazines. He has worked as Features Editor with the Press Trust of India, as International Editor for *Indian Express* and as the South Asia correspondent with *Asian Leader*, a leading British newspaper. He has been extensively published in various journals and has officiated on the jury of several national and international film festivals. His authored books include *Bollywood Unplugged: Deconstructing Cinema in Black and White; Kishore Kumar: Method in Madness; Bollywood Uncensored: What You Don't See on Screen and Why;* and *Everybody Wants Hits: 10 Mantras of Success in Bollywood Cinema.*

Apart from his love for cinema, Derek Bose is a keen Sunday painter and has directed several short films including the award-winning documentary, *Dance of the Gods.*

ST GEORGE'S
SCHOOL LIBRARY
NEWPORT, R.I.

St. George's School

3 3784 00050 6311